Thg/June 1991 vol XCIV 759

By ANDREW NORMAN SPCK 1990 ix + 142 pp.

...ned attempt to restate the traditional spirituality
...hin the boundaries set up by academic theology
...ry emphasis on practical experience versus
... The author starts with three ordinary ex-
...hich is in some way numinous. He goes on to
...ualities of silence as we experience it in
...ellectual enquiry, reflective ways of being
...olation brought about by suffering; how
...pon in modern philosophical and theolo-
...red as a means of approaching God in
...and mystical teaching.
...arefully argued. The shadow side is that
...emphasis on spirituality as a process of
...y to caricature attitudes to prayer and
...with the author's own. The advantage is
...ntellectual honesty with strong feeling and
...of prayer has a cumulative impact which
...e chapter on suffering for example, in real

CHRISTOPHER MOODY

Silence in God

Silence in God

ANDREW NORMAN

First published in Great Britain 1990
SPCK
Holy Trinity Church
Marylebone Road
London NW1 4DU

Thanks are due to Gwydion Thomas for permission to reproduce the extract from
'Kneeling' by R. S. Thomas, in his *Selected Poems* (Newcastle upon Tyne,
Bloodaxe, 1986).

British Library Cataloguing in Publication Data

Norman, Andrew *1954–*
  Silence in God.
  1. Christian life. Prayer. Silence
  I. Title
  248.32

ISBN 0–281–04477–5

Phototypeset by J&L Composition Ltd, Filey, North Yorkshire
Printed in Great Britain by Dostesios Printers Ltd, Trowbridge, Wilts.

Contents

Hush, be still; welcome!
Older than the mountains, purer than the sky.
In the beginning; silence.
We cover you over and hide from you.
But you are here, always, for us;
you – silence – You.

We scrabble in the dust,
thinking to strain the dust for eternal gold.
But you are here:
form of the formed,
breath of the breathing,
presence of the quiet earth.

Names for you we utter,
each time grander and more fitting.
These names, neither accepted nor rejected,
sink deep into our minds,
rooting in forgetfulness,
until, suddenly, we are named!

We want to hear the message,
and we want to preach it boldly.
We want the substance, the reward,
a reason for the effort.
We want, we want.
Silence is the message, for what we need
is to wait.

But, O, the emptiness of your namelessness.
Against you we rail:
O cry of the forsaken,
vain hope of the hopeless,
bitterness of the despairing,
begging bowl of the dying;
we lash out,
and your bruised body twitches.

Tears drying, uncertain peace returns.
Unlocking hardened hearts,
stilling, with a single outstretched arm
all the winds and waves.
The empty heart opened
echoes to an eternal silence –

like finding like!
Peace passing understanding: home.

Hush, be still.
Impregnated with silence
we carry
the Word.

ANDREW NORMAN

Foreword

It is, I believe, a fundamental fact of human existence that we are all being drawn to God. My interest in the theme of silence derives from this personal dynamic – and is offered to others who are discovering that they are themselves secretly involved in that most tremendous mystery of the God in Christ who reaches out to humankind. In the stillness of our hearts we touch a quietness quite beyond ourselves. This silence both calms and challenges us, is balm and bane: it strips us naked and asks for the fullest response.

It is a feature of our day that we write and think much about prayer, but pray too little. Silence, whether in the liturgy or as private contemplation, is a helpful antidote to our intellectual activism. But it will turn out to be an extremely hard way to follow to the end – certainly it is not the most comfortable form of Christian prayer. Nevertheless I believe that it is a most appropriate form of prayer for a secular age which yet looks for a 'spirituality' since it requires both a rigorous honesty and the rediscovery of our religious traditions.

I am heavily indebted to those who have been patient enough to encourage and guide me in my own little pilgrimage of faith: Fr Ernest Chown and the church of St Andrew, Worthing; Canon John Dilnot; Dr Grace Jantzen of King's College, London; and my wife, Jacky, without whom I should be lost.

Andrew Norman
March 1990

ix

1 · *In the Beginning: Silence*

'The Lord is here!' So the Anglicans of our day often confidently affirm when they gather to celebrate the Eucharist according to the Alternative Service Book. Some may think it a facile modern version of the primitive invocation, 'Dominus vobiscum'. Others can see it as a little indication of a renewed appreciation of both sacrament and community in the life of the Church. But it might be that the directness of this new liturgical call reflects a certain quality of experience which, apparently lacking in the modern world, is urgently looked for – and indeed by many more people than those who regularly take part in church worship. Is it not the case that a sense of God's presence continues to matter to many people, including some who would certainly not describe themselves as being particularly 'religious'? The threat of AIDS, the spectre of mass starvation in developing nations, and our capacity to destroy both the environment and ourselves may seem to indicate that we live in a godforsaken world. Yet at a certain primal level of human experience the sense of God's presence continues to be discovered.

I shall not attempt to prove this claim. One reads the latest religious opinion polls and is pleased when they seem to offer support. The 'hunches' of those whose business it is to know the beliefs prevalent in our society should also be attended to. For example, the former Head of Religious Broadcasting for the BBC, David Winter, ventured the following asertion:

> If there is one thing more than any other that I have learned from my seventeen years in religious broadcasting, it is that Christianity in Britain amounts to much more than the sum total of church-going. ... Modern Britain is not, by and large, a churchgoing society, but it is very far from being a secular one ... The vast majority of British people say they believe in God, and it is sectarianism of the worst kind that dismisses such a claim as meaningless.[1]

Such a claim may be measured against statistical evidence and achieve some degree of verification, but for me the bedrock of its truth is a belief in the reality and universal availability of God. The first and last term of our exploration here will be the acknowledgement of God's real presence – an objective presence that *all* people have an opportunity to know subjectively for themselves. Caroline Stephen, a nineteenth-century Quaker (and the aunt of Virginia Woolf), articulated this same conviction when she explained what was for her, too, 'the one corner-stone of belief'.

> God does indeed communicate with each one of the spirits he has made, in a direct and living inbreathing of some measure of the breath of his own life; ... he never leaves himself without a witness in the heart as well as in the surroundings of man; and ... in order clearly to hear the divine voice thus speaking to us we need to be still; to be alone with him in the secret place of his presence; ... all flesh should keep silence before him.[2]

Certainly not all Christians would agree with this, and I do not wish to imply that all who experience the Divine presence have experience of the same type or degree. But it is a fact that we clergy frequently encounter individuals (often indeed beyond the ambit of church life) who have a deep sense of God. It is very rewarding to mull over some of the things that are characteristically admitted in such conversations. But I wish first to explain what I mean by 'a sense of God's presence'. Since it might seem a rather diffuse subjective experience, let us allow the words of one man to evoke its quality for us. For almost 200 years the writings on this subject of a Carmelite lay-brother, Brother Lawrence, have been widely valued. Nicholas Herman, formerly footman and then soldier, became Brother Lawrence at the Carmelite monastery in seventeenth-century Paris, and was set to work in the kitchen. The Lord, for Brother Lawrence, was to be found there, even in the very mundane work of preparing food. 'The time of business does not with me differ from the time of prayer; and in the noise and clatter of my kitchen, while several persons are at the same time calling for different things, I possess God in as great tranquillity as if I were upon my knees at the blessed sacrament.'[3]

Brother Lawrence may be called a mystic, but he was not the sort to describe his experience in high-flown, esoteric terms. He referred to God as a good and faithful Friend who was continually present, and with whom he could converse quite easily. Brother Lawrence encouraged the correspondents whom he attracted to think of God in this way themselves, knowing from his own experience that this approach would deepen their sense of God's presence. It is only natural for us, he taught, 'to act with God in the greatest simplicity, speaking to Him frankly and plainly, and imploring His assistance in our affairs, just as they happen'. Since for Brother Lawrence God was present within and throughout his menial work in the kitchen, there could be little qualitative distinction between work and prayer. The presence of God was all in all. We are told that he kept to the monastic timetable of prayer, not because he felt any need to do so to find God, but simply out of obedience to his religious superior! Even in the busiest moments he felt close to God. He wrote, indeed, in one letter: 'It is not necessary for being with God to be always at church. We may make an oratory of our heart wherein to retire from time to time to converse with Him in meekness, humility, and love. Everyone is capable of such familiar conversation with God, some more, some less.'

This question of the *necessity* of church worship for those with a religious faith has a very contemporary ring. Parish clergy are continually encountering people who claim the name of 'Christian', but then confess they feel no need to attend church. As I say, what seems to matter more for such people is an abiding sense of the presence of God – wherever they are. One wonders what the Church's response to this should be, especially when we hear it being said of Brother Lawrence, 'That he was more united to God in his outward employments than when he left them for devotion and retirement.'

However, it is important that the full range of Brother Lawrence's teaching be heard. His was no facile message concerning a God who is casually ever-present in an undemanding way. If he affirms our general experience, he also challenges us to appreciate its deeper implications. Above all, he says that it is God's love for us that accounts for his presence. In coming to know him we have not achieved anything of ourselves, for he first reached out to us. This love appeals for our response. So Brother Lawrence uses the image of a baby feeding at his mother's breast. Attending to the presence of God we shall find a sweetness and delight, and at the same time be nurtured and fed by the Lord. But this love is not simply to be taken on demand. We are invited to enter into a reciprocal relationship in which we shall find ourselves tested. There will, he warns, certainly be moments of dryness, insensibility and irksomeness. The sense of God's presence leads inevitably to the frustrations of a personal aridity in which God may even seem to be quite absent. Of course, we eventually come to realize that this has all been for the good. The relationship has grown and matured. A mere sense of Divine presence is on the way to being refined into a fully responsive relationship.

Could it really be that Brother Lawrence articulates that experience of the presence of God which is common, in varying degrees, to many people still? He certainly uses a plain language that is accessible, speaking of God as a Friend who is universally available. But although he has a light touch, he does not veil the demands that this divine love will make on those who do respond – and perhaps this is not so readily acceptable! Perhaps the quality that has caused his lucid writings to be appreciated for so long as a spiritual classic is the sense that he uncovers something that is at once profoundly simple and of the highest value for us all. This pearl of great price creates a condition of inner resolution. There is a liberation from mundane anxieties as one is warmed from within: 'I make it my business only to persevere in His holy presence, wherein I keep myself by a simple attention, and a general fond regard to God, which I may call an *actual presence* of God; or, to speak better, an habitual, silent, and secret conversation of the soul with God which often causes me joys and raptures inwardly.'

It is precisely this 'habitual, silent, and secret conversation of the soul with God' that characterizes so well the experience that I believe many of us to have, even in this apparently godless age. Admittedly Brother Lawrence speaks of it in a much more confident way than we might be able to, but the mention of silence and covertness and the sense of presence indicate a familiar experience. Three recent personal conversations help to show what I mean. The first was had with a lady, Mrs T, who is not a church member. However, she was brought up as a Roman Catholic and latterly has helped with the flower arranging at her local Anglican parish church. She shared with me her personal belief in God. 'I feel that there *is* something, whether it be a force ... certainly nothing tangible ... I do feel that there is a being of some kind that causes our destiny, that takes hold of us in certain ways – whether one wants to stand up and admit it in a gathering of people or not.'

This conviction is important for her even if its articulation was rather hesitant. She went on cautiously to describe particular moments of experience that bolstered her belief. They have some-times occurred while she was alone in church, quietly arranging flowers. 'I'll give you an example of being in a presence – which is when I do the flowers in the chancel. Now that is a very real thing to me, I *feel* it's a holy of holies, I feel somewhat privileged to be there in the first place and I do feel an *aura*.' She noted one occasion when she entered the church only to find that the flowers did not need any attention. The building was empty and silent: 'nothing needed to be done, nobody else was there, and I just *stood* by the font at the back. I don't know how long I stood there for – five or ten minutes – but that helped me.'

Mrs T used the word God, but it was the sense of presence that she really wanted to emphasize. It was obviously a significant moment, but she was wary of making too much of it. 'I don't feel I've got to experience that kind of thing on a regular basis. I feel it's a privilege when it happens and a wonderful thing but – perhaps I back away from this – maybe I'm a coward, afraid of getting too involved? I don't know.'

Perhaps, in fact, Mrs T came to recognize those personal demands that such experience makes and that Brother Lawrence warned of. At any rate, her experience can be identified as the early stirrings of that type of relationship with God that Brother Lawrence himself entered into more fully. For her too, this sense of presence is secret and silent – and in more ways than one. In the first place there is a reluctance to articulate her understanding of God. When I asked her to explain her belief further she answered, 'It's a very strange question, isn't it, how one defines it, how one explains it?' and we did not get much further. Then, secondly, the silence of the church building, in which she was alone, played a part in her account. One imagines that if the church had been milling with other flower arrangers she would have been in a quite different state of mind. Finally, there is a reluctance to dwell too long on the significance of such moments. I felt that she did not want to give the impression that they were unrelated to the rest of her life, but rather quite the opposite. She said she was helped, as if reminded that God was continuously present and did not have to be sought only in such places as that quiet chancel. This echoes Brother Lawrence's confession that he possessed God just as much in the noise and clatter of his kitchen as in the church. The sense of God's presence is hidden secretly in the warp and woof of daily life.

This element of silence and secrecy is very curious, and one wonders whether it is an integral part of such experience. A second conversation was had with a priest, but this time concerned an interesting moment in a setting that was not at all religious. I first asked the Reverend E how he personally conceived of God. He spoke of knowing God 'in the depths of my being', admitting that he did not picture God as being 'outside or elsewhere in any way'. I then asked him what prayer was for him. 'Much of my prayer, silence and words, is as much a conversation with myself – which I would go on to explain by using terms such as "God deep within me", "the ground of my being".' The conversation continued as the Reverend E reflected on the different ways in which he had been brought to a point of awareness of God. There had been moments in church worship, though perhaps not many. There had been insights received in personal relationships. Then he related something that had happened while on holiday in France:

> On holiday last year we went round a vineyard near Bordeaux which was a massive place, and entered the great cellars – which were like a cathedral, all the barrels lined up. There was actually a lot of noise that morning, the pumps were all working and it was a very noise-filled cellar with the rhythmic pumping. And in an extraordinary way – there were three or four of us there – there was no silence outside, but it was a very stilling experience for myself 'inside' that moment. It was a simple setting, nothing ornate, a simple cellar, beautiful. I felt deeply good, a rested feeling, peaceful.

One may question whether this was a religious experience at all – except that it was reported in the midst of a conversation about God! As before, the conversation opened with an unwillingness to talk 'about' God. The Reverend E explained that, for him, the identity of God is only discovered as one enters into the reality of one's own self. Thus, the journey is a personal one, and its insights not easily expressed to others. But, unlike the experience described in the first conversation, this one did not occur in a silent place. In fact, exteriorly there was much noise, and the only silence was that of an interior quality. It was a stillness, a being at rest and a sense of peace – and it reminded me of that tranquillity that Brother Lawrence described. Like Mrs T, the Reverend E stressed that this particular experience did not denote a hiatus in the flow of ordinary life, but was very much part of its continuing pattern, while perhaps reflecting its deeper meaning. So, once more, silence played its part in the tale. A presence, about whom one can say little in an objective, impersonal way, is appreciated momentarily as an inner stillness, and one's whole person is calmed and reassured. There is not a great deal to report, but something important has happened.

Very often, however, even committed Christians are unable to refer to particular moments of religious experience. They will explain that their faith in God has grown gradually, and that the sense of his presence remains continuous rather than episodic. This was what Mrs B shared with me. I knew her to have struggled slowly and somewhat painfully towards an acceptance of the Christian faith – and I knew too something of the peace and joy that this had brought her. When, however, I asked her about God, she spoke of the need to be involved with the whole human family. 'What about God though?' I pressed. She replied:

Oh well, there's no great light shining, no vision of God. I just feel that there *is* something which really does affect us all – in different ways because we are different personalities.

Faith is … well, a being in tune with God. I try not to be pretentious, but it's a being in harmony with the whole community. You see, this is one of my big worries that so many people are *not* in harmony with one another, and this goes on in ever increasing circles …

I think that by trying to shut out the 'outside' people, by trying to remain in their tight knit community, they lose out a lot, they even try to shut out God, but God is still there anyway.

Mrs B feels she encounters God's presence through a committed involvement with other people. She speaks therefore as if this presence is a universal quality which is diffused throughout human society. To deny part of the human family is to deny God himself. Her recognition of this presence, and her eventual response to it, has given her a tranquillity that she positively radiates. But in our conversation I felt quite strongly her reluctance to abstract the presence from the concrete situation of which, for her, it is such an important quality. God is met as one gives oneself to others, for God is thoroughly involved in human life and calls for our involvement too. Thus it is participation rather than any objective analysis that will sensitize us to his presence.

The element of silence once again characterizes this experience. God's presence is real enough to Mrs B, but it is hidden in the interplay of human relationships. His presence is indeed the secret that validates and grants the deepest meaning to our dealings with one another. God as an objective entity is silent; the sense of his presence is to be lived and subjectively appropriated. It is clear to her friends that Mrs B has herself grown into a state of being that might be described as an inner stillness or peace.

In these conversations with very ordinary people about their spiritual feelings, the theme of silence emerged time and time again. There is the silence that is a reluctance or an inability to articulate one's personal notion of 'God'. Particular moments of religious experience occur in a quiet and peaceful location – or at least induce an inner quiescence. Then there is the silence of God who seems to saturate the whole of human experience, and who therefore cannot be pointed to as 'here' if that means not 'there'. For each of these three people with whom I talked, the presence of God is highly significant – and in wider conversations one gains the impression that this appreciation transcends the boundaries of institutional Christianity. Correspondingly, in one form or another silence seems to be a common characteristic of their experience. This makes one wonder exactly what sort of connection there can be between the keeping of silence and a sense of God's presence. Brother Lawrence certainly felt there was. 'I do not advise you to use multiplicity of words in prayer', he wrote, 'many words and long discourses being often the occasions of wandering. Hold yourself in prayer before God like a dumb or paralytic beggar at a rich man's gate. Let it be your business to keep you mind in the presence of the Lord.' Moreover, in recent years there has been a whole spate of popular books exploring the value of a contemplative type of prayer for those committed to an active life. Silence has almost become a buzz word of contemporary spirituality. One does not, however, have to become a mystic to appreciate the religious value of silence.

Mrs T, the flower arranger, has grown to love the quietness of an empty church. Church buildings, particularly rural ones, are often oases of silence in a world that grows increasingly noisy and frenetic. Shutting the church door behind you, especially if you are alone, is sometimes to enter a quietness that is in itself highly evocative of religious meaning. R. S. Thomas, Welshman, priest and poet, knows this feeling:

> Moments of great calm,
> Kneeling before an altar
> Of wood in a stone church
> In summer, waiting for the God
> To speak; the air a staircase
> For silence . . . [4]

But what is happening? We leave the church feeling renewed and at peace, feeling indeed that there has been a movement towards God. The poet refers to this peace, but implies that it has a potential significance greater than that of a mere welcome relief from noise. The silence is a waiting for God to speak, an invitaton to ascend the staircase. It is as if the quietness of the empty church stills our human preoccupations and then begins to suggest itself as the very medium for intimations of God's presence. The silence calms and becomes *the* Calm.

It *is* possible, from time to time, for a special peace to descend on the home. I write with the sounds of our four-month-old daughter ringing in my ears! But there are moments when baby and new father catch each other's eye and simply gaze silently in mutual wonder and curiosity. An elderly couple sitting comfortably before the fire, the one quietly knitting, the other reading a newspaper, might not exchange any words for a long period. But there may be a strong feeling of security and warmth, the two being fully 'present' to each other. An intimate candlelit dinner does not necessarily require sustained intelligent conversation for romance to flourish. The meaning of those glances and the sense of expectancy fills the silence with import. The refraining from casual talk itself becomes an effective means for conveying what is felt.

It is in similar moments of domestic quiet that God's presence can be felt. As you do the washing-up, mechanically wiping the plates and stacking them on one side, so the mind is free for a consciousness of God to dawn. If the rest of the family go out for the evening and you are left alone, then your attention may quite naturally settle down to an appreciation of the more than superficial. Might it be the fact that many women end up spending long hours isolated at home for part of their lives which helps to explain why they tend to be more religiously minded than their husbands? Of course, in reality, the home is rarely what might be called a haven of silence! Even if the children are asleep, then the television will probably be on. The telephone interrupts and there is often the constant noise of traffic from the road outside. This results in our attention being shallow and caught by the immediate and the purely external. It means that we rarely have the space to think and reflect. But we are also denied contact with that quality which can itself become a medium of God's presence. Silence stills us and then grants us a new expectation. The constant pollution of extraneous noise prevents both.

We began with the new uncompromising liturgical affirmation, 'The Lord is here!' Another new – or rather, rediscovered – element of contemporary worship is the arranged period of silence. Before the collect, or prayer for the day, after the sermon, following the great Amen at the conclusion of the Eucharistic prayer, and after Holy Communion, moments of silence are suggested in the rubrics. Thus here again a sense of God's presence – 'The Lord is here' – is linked with the keeping of silence. It may be felt that these rubrics indicate a rather self-conscious concern for a quality that the more traditional services usually had quite naturally. The early-morning – 8 a.m. and Prayer Book – celebration, still surviving in most Anglican parish churches, is a typically quiet, devotional occasion, with a few individuals dotted solitarily about the building. But, contrived or not, it would seem that we cannot do without some silence in the liturgy, whether it comes as a breather in the middle of a lively Family Service, or as a moment of reflection during an intimate Eucharist. A constant diet of worship that is all words and action leaves one exhausted and denuded. Silent pauses, and these *can* occur in a natural, unselfconscious manner, help to create an appropriate atmosphere. Words, so frequently repeated, come back to life. The worshipper has the space to consider the personal implications of what is preached. A mechanical ritual glows again with a sense of encounter with God.

There has of course been a much more explicit appreciation of silence over the last two decades with the rise to popularity of contemplative-type prayer. A large number of books have been written with the aim of making this ancient form of Christian prayer accessible to modern minds. One can see the popular interest emerging in the 1960s against a background of fascination with mysticism and self-awareness. But it may be that this early dilettantism has now begun to mature into a more serious renascence of the contemplative tradition. Evidence of this is indicated by the emergence of new religious orders in which the practice of contemplative prayer has a central position. The ecumenical community of Taizé in France attracts thousands of young visitors each year. Its worship is simple, and yet highly innovative in an imaginative return to traditional liturgical sources. Word and song are held in a context of silence. In discussion, the young pilgrims are encouraged to listen – to themselves, to others, and to God. The two polarities of action and contemplation are presented as the spring of the Christian life. The Roman Catholic order 'Little Brothers of Jesus' was founded after the example of Charles de Foucauld, and is committed to bringing contemplation into the industrial workplace. Every day after work each little cell of Brothers gathers for silent prayer, and they regard this as the heart of their lives. That which they discover in the silence will, they hope, overflow and touch those ordinary men and women whom they work alongside day by day. Many ordinary parishes and local churches maintain small prayer groups. In the past, intercession would have been seen as the object of their existence. These days, their prayer is often of a silent, contemplative kind. Thus the popularity of books *about* contemplation suggests that many are indeed taking this way seriously, and finding it an appropriate form of prayer for modern people. One senses that many Christians are now bringing a more passive mode of listening and receptiveness to their time of prayer.

If 'silence' has become a buzz word in our current spiritual vocabulary, then we must acknowledge that it is a compendious term. There are different sorts of silence in different forms of religious experience. The same word can refer to our stammering from having reached the limit of religious articulation as to the practice of a highly developed technique of prayer. What unites the different uses of the term is the common disposition that the different types of silence often seem to engender. This disposition is the breaking in of a sense of God's presence. Somewhere or other the quality of silence nearly always has to be brought in to complete the account of so much of one's personal encounter with God. This provokes a certain curiosity. *Why* is silence significant? We may be drawn to a silent form of prayer only to find, after some time, a questioning of the validity of this approach. *How* is silence supposed to work? Too many popular books about prayer produced in the last two decades talk blandly about silence as if it has one obvious

meaning. We will be advised to quieten down our chattering prayer.
'Be still and know that I am God.' But such advice needs unpacking.
There is a need for a more complete explanation of how the different
types of silence can help us to know God. This is what we shall hope
to begin to do here. And at the outset, a basic assumption about the
absolute centrality of silence in Christian experience must be clearly
pointed to. Certainly silence has a variety of instrumental functions.
We shall hope to identify these along the way. Some very practical
suggestions will be made as to how we might personally make more
use of silence. At the heart of this book, however, will be the claim
that in the subjective experience of silence the objective reality of
God is there to be discovered. Not only can silence mediate the
presence of God, but it can do so in such a manner that we cannot
separate God from the medium of his disclosure to us. We must not
be afraid of this spiritual blurring of the objective with the subjective, but rather attend to the mystery of God's manifestation in
our deepest selves.

Silence is of course a universal human experience, and it has
already been suggested that the spiritual awareness that it prompts is
more widely appreciated than might be acknowledged. But there is
another universal factor that conditions most human experience
in our Western, industrialized world. This is the criterion of
empiricism. Reliable knowledge, it lays down, comes through our
five senses. True facts are those elements of our experience that can
be measured, repeatedly tested, and that are consistent with the rest
of our knowledge. Hard-nosed practitioners of this approach would
seem likely to laugh in the face of the sort of 'mysticism' we have
begun to explore. Already we have spoken of our *sense* of God and of
our *feeling* his presence. Where, we might be asked, are the data of
such experience? Neither Brother Lawrence, nor any of the three
people with whom I conversed, referred to visions or heavenly
voices. All they had to describe was something intensely personal
and unquantifiable. At first sight, it would seem that there were, in
empirical terms, no data.

This brings us to the impasse that occurred when empiricist
thinkers brought their theory of knowledge to bear on religious
beliefs. That questioning began most decisively in the period of the
Enlightenment, but the conflict continues into our own day. We
shall see in later chapters that empiricism has indeed been criticized
on philosophical grounds and incorporated into more sophisticated

theories. But its central principle is still very much taught and accepted in our society. We *know* a fact when we receive data of it, and when those data can be demonstrated to others. Now the apparent lack of demonstrable data in personal religious experience has been seized upon by certain thinkers. For example, back in the 1930s a young Oxford lecturer, A. J. Ayer, made the influential assertion that a particular statement is only open to being proved true when it can be said what specific observations would do so. The trouble with religious statements, as he pointed out, is that some believers continue to believe *whatever* happens. This is no problem, such believers might well retort, for our convictions about God are of a wholly different order to mundane, this-worldly knowledge. Hans Küng, a Roman Catholic theologian, seems to make this point in the course of his own research for the meaning of God. 'God's existence is not empirically ascertainable, it is not there to be discovered in space and time; God would not be God if man could perceive and observe him with his own senses at certain places and certain times.'[5]

We can imagine A. J. Ayer smiling wryly at this. If God is quite remote from any demonstrable data then theology must remain an elaborate hypothesis. It follows that one must refrain from judging the claims of those who say they have experienced God. By their own admission, the experience has no grounds. But this leaves contemporary believers in a very insecure position. There are moments when it seems to us that we experience God. Christians indeed feel a great deal of anxiety through being caught in this conflict between belief and the modern understanding of fact. But we should not feel too defensive, for it may be that the latter approach is able to stimulate a renewed understanding of what is actually happening in religious experience. We are urged to reveal the data of our experiences. Very well, there is often the element of silence. We do not see God's face, we may not hear his voice, but very often the silence itself is quite tangible and substantial. We must explore the possibility that silence is the demonstrable data of those times when we sense the presence of God.

There is much to commend a spirituality that begins by taking seriously the familiar features of our everyday world. Having our feet on the ground helps to check that self-indulgent theorizing that separates prayer from action, contemplation from practical involvement. But we must not forget that if there are, after all, some demonstrable data of our encounter with God, then they are certainly received in a peculiar manner. Hans Küng throws out a clue to this in his use of the term 'meta-empirical': 'a meta-empirical that does not lie behind, beyond, above, outside this reality, but – so to speak – constitutes the inner aspect of present reality'. Rather than seeking to work against the grain of much modern thought, let us accept the influence of empiricism as we explore the meaning of our sense of God's presence. It may sound rather an unusual suggestion, but since we are directed to look for demonstrable data, let us consider the silence itself as being such. Küng's term 'meta-empirical' encourages us to deepen our understanding of the sort of data that would be received in experience of God. So let us look for data that somehow relate to 'the inner aspect of present reality'.

Someone might argue that this is merely playing with words. Surely the term 'silence' does not describe anything real that exists and can be experienced? Is it not in fact merely a negative description indicating the absence of anything and a failure to experience? Now, of course, silence may simply refer to a lack of any sound, revealing a vacuum. In books about contemplative prayer, both those classical works written by the mystics of the Church and modern popular paperbacks, the language *is* often unclear. It is implied that the silence to be entered into represents a complete nothingness – which, if true, would lead to a ridiculously frustrating experience! But if, say, colour is a real datum, or odour, then silence may be just as certain a characteristic of some entity of which we feel we have reliable experience. As with other data, it is up to us to interpret and work out its significance. Silence may be solemn and stern, or warm and loving. We all know from our own experience, if we think about it, that silence can indeed speak volumes. It is often one element among others to be assessed in a particular encounter with another person.

However, there is a very important sense in which silence may indeed be a mark of very negative religious experience. In times of crisis, people turn to God for help, but it is not everyone who feels they get a response. When a dearly loved son is killed in a motorcycle accident the anguished parents ask a metaphysical 'Why?' There is often no satisfactory answer. It would seem to them that God chooses to remain silent, and this deathly hush is very bitter. If it is true that many people, and not just church members, have a deep and often unspoken appreciation of the continual presence of God, then the opposite would also seem to be true too. Any priest can think of individuals who would dearly love to believe in God, but in their heart of hearts feel that the cosmos is empty of any Deity. Instead of a reassuring sense of God's presence, there is for such people often only a deafening silence. The awful suffering that was endured in the concentration camps of the Second World War formed a human crucible in which this despair before God's silence was most definitively realized. The Chosen People felt totally abandoned, their prayers for help apparently falling on deaf ears. We cannot consider the relevance of silence in religious experience without returning to this moment of Jewish history, for it has a universal human significance.

Furthermore, we must try to avoid romanticizing contemplative prayer. It may, in the first instance, be relaxing to rest in the stillness. But, before long, we will discover that we have entered into a desert – which is an extremely uncompromising environment for prayer. I recall from the conversations alluded to earlier, that although silence, in different respects, characterized their experiences, the individuals concerned also expressed the feeling that silence was far from being always congenial. Mrs T said, 'I'm not the sort of person that likes silence really. I get up in the morning and the first thing I do is to turn the radio on ... I seek companionship always.' Most of us will understand what she means. Despite all the positive things that can be said about peace and quiet, the silence of an empty house, for example, can be very oppressive. A too-self-conscious practising of contemplative prayer may also become stultifying if the technique begins to obscure the object of the exercise. The Reverend E implied that contemplation should be entered into spontaneously, and admitted that at times he felt a formal and disciplined practice to be unhelpful. He belongs to a local contemplative prayer cell:

The last occasion I went actually just nothing was happening, nothing worked for me that morning, I might just as well have not been there. It was doing nothing for me at all, it didn't even still me in any way, I was just a restless person when I went in and a restless person when I came out. I think I'd have done better to have gone down to the Marsh and walked by our little church there. And actually I think that's a feeling which a large number of people would have.

Silence is indeed often a harsh environment. In it, the reality of ourselves tends to be exposed. We feel questioned and tested by it. We shall have to remember that it is not the easiest form of Christian prayer, and may not lead to the most comfortable of experiences.

Nevertheless, it is my hope that this book will offer some encouragement for us to enter bravely into that environment. I ask for patience and endurance from the reader, particularly over the next couple of chapters. Nothing will be said that will not become clear after a little thought, and perhaps the use of a dictionary. The effort that may be required will be worthwhile. A mature spirituality demands some tough thinking and will inevitably raise questions not susceptible to a quick answer. But my intention is not merely to present a few abstract ideas which are rather remote from the practice of a Christian life, but ultimately to suggest some practical ways in which we might discover God afresh. To this end, the theme of each chapter will be channelled into a specific form of silent prayer. Underlying our exploration of silence so far has been the principle that experience of the presence of God is universally and freely available to all. The Quaker Caroline Stephen referred to that 'direct and living inbreathing of some measure of the breath of his own life' which God has with 'each one of the spirits he has made'. But the immediacy of this experience does not guarantee an instant ability to cope with it and appreciate it to the full. God may be close to each one of us, but we have to allow ourselves sufficient time and space for this realization to dawn. My three personal conversations were glimpses into how people sometimes encounter God in some sort of wordless stillness. But they also revealed that such experience may be confusing – and perhaps almost too intense. Mrs T, for example, was quite wary: 'I feel it's a privilege when it happens and a wonderful thing, but ... perhaps I back away from this ... maybe I'm a coward ... afraid of getting too involved? I don't know.'

Perhaps it is just better if we allow ourselves to enter more gently into this form of awareness. Silence *is* a harsh environment. Brother Lawrence makes a sensible guide. He suggests that we approach God in the easiest and most natural manner – by simply reaching out to him in the here-and-now, accepting totally his presence with us at all times: 'We ought to act with God in the greatest simplicity, speaking to Him frankly and plainly, and imploring His assistance in our affairs, just as they happen'. This is not a difficult thing to do. The only problem is that it seems *too* easy. We expect prayer to require heroic self-discipline and to lead to the experience of profound things. But even a child could pray like this, chattering away to the Heavenly Father. Brother Lawrence had the maturity to realize that this simple relating of ourselves to God was the right way to enter into the inner stillness of spiritual recollection. We should not despise this child-like form of prayer, for it will enable us to interpret the silence to which it ultimately leads in a manner that is far from childish.

Here is a prayer for us all to practise *now*: 'Father . . .' It is a most positive point of entry into silence, and it will enable us to sustain prayer in silence, silence *as* prayer. Finally we must be ready at all times to return to this simple, humble talking to God when we feel, as we inevitably shall sometimes, that faith has lost all meaning.

Notes

1 D. Winter, *Battered Bride*. Eastbourne, Monarch, 1988, p. 181.
2 C. Stephen, 'Quaker Strongholds', *Quaker Spirituality*, ed. D. V. Steere, London, SPCK, 1984, p. 246.
3 Brother Lawrence, *The Practice of the Presence of God*. New Jersey, Spire Books, 1976, p. 29.
4 R. S. Thomas, from 'Kneeling', in his *Selected Poems*. Newcastle upon Tyne, Bloodaxe, 1986.
5 H. Küng, *Does God Exist?* London, Collins, 1980, pp. 549–50.

2 · *Presence of the Quiet Earth*

There are days when life seems utterly commonplace. One follows the same routine – meals, work, rest, television. Familiar faces appear again across breakfast table and office desk as humdrum, predictable conversations are re-run. Monotonous, overcast weather, or perhaps the prosaic, soulless vista of a housing estate, will seem to underline a flat, insipid quality of life. Increasing standardization intensifies the dullness. Soon hardly any corner of the world will be beyond the reach of satellite television, while already similar cars are driven in universally crowded city streets, and we are all preoccupied with the same international affairs. More and more do people move into a uniform, suburban existence. At times this sense of the mundane can become quite oppressive.

Yet this is rarely the whole story. In our personal lives certain situations arise, apparently spontaneously, that excite, rejuvenate – and indeed may also frighten us. We fall in love. We become ill. We are offered a new job. We move house. Then everything is suddenly different. We have to form a fresh personal perspective. Collectively too, we are at intervals reminded that the stability of this world is purely relative. The sudden *coup d'état* or the diplomatic crisis can trigger an escalation of tension with unforeseen consequences. Since we directly experience such a small segment of the time scale of our planet's evolution, it is easy for us to imagine that things in the natural world are now as they were in the beginning and ever shall be. All the more disconcerting is the moment when it suddenly impinges on the public consciousness that our weather pattern, for example, is fundamentally changing. The reality is that human existence is a precarious raft of stability swirling on a sea of change. The relative firmness allows us to settle into conservative thoughts and habitual behaviour. But the familiar ordinariness will at times be assaulted by a glimpse of the wider reality. We may fall easily into the contentments of a daily routine with its creature comforts – and then read somewhere that we are actually part of a cosmos in which the galaxies are rushing away from the big bang at almost the speed of light. Our sphere of daily experience seems then of extremely minor significance. A sense of the extra-mundane breaks in upon what can seem, at times, an almost total ordinariness.

Nothing is more ordinary than silence. We endure it in the bus to work because no one wants to speak. It settles over the house at night as everyone lies asleep. The cleaner knows it as he works his way around the office desks before the typewriters begin their clattering again. This sort of silence does not seem worthy of our attention. It is just there – or, rather, nothing is there for the moment. We may try to break it by saying something witty or interesting, but most of the time we just accept it. Silence is a mundane characteristic of our ordinary lives, though most of it gets filled up. But it is precisely this silence, this ordinary absence of any meaningful sound, which may be the occasion for a breaking-in of the extraordinary.

Bread, too, is a mundane substance. On its own it is a rather plain and unexciting food, and we may not be able to afford jam every day. We eat it to live, and if we do think of anything as we munch it, it will be of those who lack even this basic necessity. Yet is is this very ordinary food that is treated with such reverence in the Christian Eucharist – as more modern hymns emphasize. For example, 'In the Lord's Service bread and wine are offered/that Christ may take them, bless them, break and give them/to all his people, his own life imparting/food everlasting.'[1] The bread *becomes*, as we say with varying degrees of emphasis, the body of Christ. As quite ordinary bread is blessed, broken and eaten, the presence of Christ is made real to the worshippers. With this mundane substance, the extra-mundane breaks in.

It is not only bread of course that is used in this way. The common substances of water and oil, as well as ordinary physical touch, are also invested with an extra-mundane significance in the Christian sacraments. Through something this-worldly, the presence and power of God breaks in upon the worshippers. The definition of a sacrament presented in the Prayer Book Catechism affirms both the mundane and the extra-mundane aspects of a sacramental event:

Question: What meanest thou by this word *Sacrament*? *Answer*: I mean an outward and visible sign of an inward and spiritual grace given unto us, ordained by Christ himself, as a means whereby we receive the same, and a pledge to assure us thereof. *Question*: How many parts are there in a Sacrament? *Answer*: Two; the outward visible sign, and the inward spiritual grace.

This is exactly the way plain ordinary silence sometimes becomes the means for an extraordinary experience. We heard in the last chapter how silence could be a very significant element of certain religious experiences. Mrs T sensed the presence of God in a quiet, empty church; the Reverend E felt 'deeply good, a rested feeling, peaceful' in a moment of inner stillness; Mrs B discerned God as the One who secretly participates in human society. Then for all three there was also that silence of being reluctant, or unable, to articulate their personal notion of 'God'. Wondering what the connection was between silence and a sense of God's presence, I suggested that the former was not only a means of prayer but could actually *be* the presence of God. These various types of silence mediate the presence of God, and in such a way that we cannot separate God from the medium of his disclosure to us. The definition of a sacrament can be used to explain this silence. The datum consists of a lack of noise, thought, or speech; this is the outward and visible sign. The meaning of this datum is the sense of God's presence; this is the inward and spiritual grace. However we become silent – whether it be through entering an empty church, or as an inner stilling of the mind; whether it represents our human inadequacy faced with the mystery of the concept of 'God', or as a sense of the ubiquitous involvement of God everywhere – the data point sacramentally beyond themselves. Hans Küng's use of the term 'meta-empirical' was quoted: 'that does not lie behind, beyond, above, outside this reality, but – so to speak – constitutes the inner aspect of present reality'.[2] The datum of silence is the present reality, and its inner aspect, if we can but discern it, is the presence of God.

It *is* a shock when we realize how infinitesimally small our sphere of experience is when compared with the scale of the known universe. The familiar is set within the context of great unfamiliarity. Our emotional selves too, though apparently well balanced and self-contained, are easily upset by the introduction of new factors from without. We have always to be open to the possibility of new personal developments. The known remains a small reserve within a larger unknown. This is the nature of all human experience, and, at the most ultimate level, it is the manner in which we experience

God. Our day-to-day lives are lived in the context of the eternal. Much of the time we may be unaware of the greater reality – even if our own limited sphere would be meaningless without it. But, just occasionally, and perhaps for some people more than others, the eternal shines through the ordinary. The monotony of the mundane is shot through with a ray of light from its all-encompassing Mystery. This is the sacramental significance that silence may come to have. The very ordinary suddenly reveals the extraordinary.

The Prayer Book Catechism defines a sacrament in a neat formula that was designed to be easily memorized. But the nature of a sacrament is not so easily grasped, for our minds tend to slip and slide on the idea that mundane matter both points to, and effectively becomes, a Divine reality – while itself remaining mundane! The more clearly we can make sense of this, however, the better we will be able to appreciate how it is that contemplative silence both mediates and *is* the presence of God. It is not too difficult to appreciate the sacraments as *signs*. Jesus himself took the bread and in breaking it prefigured the breaking of his body on the cross. Even if the disciples did not fully understand it at the Last Supper, the meaning was plain in retrospect. Similarly, washing with water is a good, clear representation of our being cleansed from sin. Bread, wine and water point fairly obviously to that which they are supposed figuratively to refer. Signs have to be appropriate if they are going to work. International road signs have been refined over the years to ensure that they are easily recognizable. Seeing a curve bent slightly to the left on a road sign immediately alerts one to the direction of the road ahead. The connection is obvious.

Of course, the term 'sacrament' cannot be used to explain contemplative silence in exactly the way that it is used in relation to baptism and the Eucharist. The practice of silent prayer was not instituted by Jesus, and has not received the Church's validation as being of normative significance for all Christians. But from the first, silence has been an element of both private prayer and public worship. In the Gospels, too, we repeatedly hear of Jesus seeking a quiet refuge in which to pray alone (Luke 6.12 for example). More important, silence is an *appropriate* form with which to signify the presence of God. Our silence points to the presence of the Other; there is quietness because we are not alone. When visitors enter a magnificent limestone cavern, such as at Cheddar Gorge, conversation dies away. A sense of the beauty, age and total 'otherness' of this subterranean world to their normal environment silences them. The silence signifies their response. Other people coming into the cave will be alerted by this silence to the realization that there is something special to be seen there. Silence may of course signify plain inattention, as in daydreaming, or the absence of anything to recognize. But it is not uncommon to find silence referring to some kind of presence. Coming across someone who looks as though he is concentrating yet is silent, we will want to know what he has just heard, or what it is he is looking at. If the bread broken at the Last Supper clearly signifies the crucified body of Christ, then silence can just as plainly be used to refer to the presence of God.

But the sacraments are not only signs of that to which they refer; they also mediate these realities. The 'outward and visible sign' is the 'means whereby we receive' the 'inward and spiritual grace'. So the bread and wine of the Eucharist are said to *be* the body and blood of Christ as the worshippers are involved in the liturgical celebration of his passion, death and resurrection. The difficulty is in explaining *how* Christians conceive the spiritual grace to be mediated by the visible sign. The theologian Paul Tillich, considering the sacrament of baptism, suggests three possible ways.[3] The first, which he calls making 'a symbolic–metaphoric interpretation of the element', makes the sacrament little more than a visual aid. 'On this inter- pretation, sprinkling by water or baptism by immersion serves the purpose of setting forth in an understandable picture the idea that is expressed also by the accompanying word. The act of baptism is thus a visible representation of the idea of baptism.' As Tillich points out, other visual aids could well be used to represent what is going on. He suggests the alternative pictures of a person passing through fire, or going down into a cave – which are indeed used in some primitive religions. The problem with this explanation is the lack of any intrinsic relationship between the outward sign and the inward grace. To interpret silence in this way would be to confine its sacramental significance to being a pictorial representation of the idea of God's presence.

The second possibility Tillich names a '*ritualistic* interpretation of the element'. This is to emphasize the divine command to perform the sacrament. 'Because of this command, water acquires its sacra- mental significance as soon as it is employed in the properly celebrated rite of baptism.' Jesus did not specifically command Christians to pray in silence. This would surely be to stretch the injunction to 'go into your room and shut the door', in Matthew 6.6, a bit too far.

Tillich's third possible interpretation lays more emphasis on the natural element of water itself. 'A special character or quality, a power of its own, is attributed to water. By virtue of this natural power, water is suited to become the bearer of a sacral power and thus also to become a sacramental element.' It may sound strange in our technological world, in which water is an element to be quantified and a resource to be used, to suggest that water 'is suited to become the bearer of a sacral power', but perhaps that merely shows the poverty of modern sensibilities. Tillich approves of this interpretation, for to his mind it does full justice to the nature of a sacrament. It affirms that the connection between the visible sign and the spiritual grace is not merely an arbitrary one.

This is not to suggest that some natural elements have a special magical quality. Certainly the offering of food, washing with water, and indeed the observing of silence, are all to be found in many other religious traditions as well as the Christian. But the emphasis in Tillich's thought, which I also wish to stress, is on the special way in which these things may be experienced. The claim is that certain things more than others are able to trigger off a particular human awareness of the Divine. The actual thing experienced, be it bread, water or silence, is only important in so far as it becomes the occasion for a greater experience of a reality beyond itself. It becomes the vehicle for the experience of that to which, as a sign, it refers. Thus something mundane enables the extra-mundane to break in upon us. Tillich invented the term 'self-transcendent realism' to express the idea that ordinary data, the here-and-now, are sometimes able to point beyond themselves to God:

> The ultimate power of being, the ground of reality, appears in a special moment, in a concrete situation, revealing the infinite depth and the eternal significance of the present. ... It is as in a thunderstorm at night, when the lightning throws a blinding clarity over all things, leaving them in complete darkness the next moment. When reality is seen in this way with the eye of a self-transcending realism, it has become something new.

A rather crude visual analogy to this experience can be drawn with our being shown one of those trick pictures in which two images can be seen. Looked at one way a cup with handles appears, but looked at again the picture seems to be of two heads facing each other. So a person entirely ignorant of the Christian faith when attending a Eucharist will witness only the ritual consumption of bread and wine. The person of faith experiences bread and wine too – and so much more. In contemplative prayer the silence is often just ordinary silence. It can be extremely boring, or in fact rather relaxing. It may be the opportunity for some personal reflection, or for the building of some elaborate theoretical house of cards. But, now and again, the silence will become self-transcending. The reality of God, of whose tender presence it is such an appropriate sign, actually breaks in upon the one who prays.

Where have we got to now? We began by examining that sense of God's presence that still seems to be available to many people in our secular society. The element of silence was seen to characterize, in different forms, three particular reported experiences. Having looked curiously at this phenomena, it was noted that modern empirical thought directs us to look for objective data to confirm the authenticity of any 'experience'. Perhaps, it was suggested, in this sort of religious experience silence is a datum? If it is so, it certainly is not interpreted in a straightforward manner. Hans Küng suggested that we have to look for data that can come to be seen as constituting 'the inner aspect of present reality'. The idea of a sacrament, familiar to most Christians, has now given us the means to make sense of Küng's suggestion. Silence in religious experience is a mundane, empirical feature of present reality. In this form, it can be taken as a sign of the quiet, loving, all-pervading presence of God. But this ordinary silence is capable of transcending itself and becoming the vehicle of a spiritual grace. It is when this happens that we need to talk about 'personal experience' of God's presence.

It may sound then as though a personal apprehension of God through silence is the easiest thing in the world. Christians ought to turn off the hymns and the sermons and tune directly into God. I do indeed wish to stress that such personal experience is more widely available than is sometimes realized. But the matter is not so simple as that. Silence is more often felt to be an experience to be avoided. We have to *learn* to appreciate that ordinary boring silence can relate to 'an inner aspect of present reality'. But for some people the 'penny will never drop'. Now this latter phrase was coined, in a religious context, by a previous (though no less adventurous) Bishop of Durham, Ian Ramsey. In his book *Religious Language*, written in

1957, he asks 'what kind of empirical anchorage have theological words?'[4] He wanted to know how our talk about God relates to our here-and-now experience of the physical world. His answer was that mundane experience occasionally produces moments of disclosure. Ordinary data prompt the disclosure of a greater dimension. The 'penny drops', 'our eyes are opened', we have a deeper appreciation. When this sort of thing happens with empirical experience, we have to use religious words to indicate that it went beyond what is normally experienced. Such words will express both its mundane and its extra-mundane aspects. As an example, Ramsey presented the word immutability when used to describe the unchanging nature of God. 'Mutable' is anchored in ordinary empirical experience, for everything we know is involved in a process of change and development. But the 'im' which qualifies this word, indicates that a particular experience of the changing world has prompted the disclosure to us of that which is eternally unchanging. He imagines how such an experience might occur:

> Let us imagine that we are travelling by train in a remote district as darkness falls. Little by little the scene is obliterated; first trees, then houses, slowly disappear from view; then the pylons, then the particular folds of the hills; then the hills themselves. Darkness has fallen: 'Fast falls the eventide'; 'the darkness deepens'. Change (if not decay) in all around I see. Now at every point in this changing scene, 'immutability', as an attribute of negative theology, whispers to us: 'But not everything changes ... Is there not something which remains invariable in the situation despite what is so visibly changing?' Such suggestions are constantly repeated as the scene constantly changes, in the hope that at some point or other the penny will drop, the ice break, the light dawn; that there will break on us that 'discernment' which is a 'sense of the unseen', a characteristically religious situation, to which 'immutability' has led us.

The term 'silence', when used in a religious context, similarly may relate to two dimensions of experience. There is ordinary silence – that which comes when the radio is turned off. Then there is a holy silence – which relates to a disclosure which may be prompted in and by the silence. Properly speaking, we should not just talk about 'silence' when thinking of it as the medium for knowing God. This term descriptive of ordinary experiences needs to be qualified. So the prophet Zechariah commands a silence of *awe*. 'Be silent, all flesh, before the Lord; for he has roused himself from his holy dwelling' (Zech. 2.13). The psalmist sings of a silence that is a *trust* in, and a *dependence* upon, the Lord. 'I have calmed and quieted my soul, like a child quieted at its mother's breast; like a child that is quieted is my soul' (Ps. 131.2). Religious silence is ordinary silence that has prompted an extraordinary disclosure, such that we need to talk about a peaceful silence, or an adoring silence – or indeed a penitential silence. The penny has dropped and the silence has brought us to an encounter with God.

Ian Ramsey became quite fascinated with religious disclosure as a psychological event. But we may well wonder what it is that causes 'the penny to drop'. One person looks at a black and white drawing and sees a cup with handles. Another looks at the same image and sees two faces. Why do they make a different judgement? A person enters an empty church one sunny afternoon and finds it a peaceful place to sit for a few moments and relax. But the silence impels another person, who enters later, to slip to her knees with a sudden sense of awe. What is it that makes them interpret the same phenomenon in a different way? The answer lies in the beliefs, the values and the expectations that they bring to the experience. We shall be examining this function in the next chapter. But it would seem that some people are easily able to see beauty, deep meaning and spiritual value in that which remains merely mundane to the rest of us. They are the natural poets, the artists and visionaries of our world.

The poet William Blake wrote in this vein to the Reverend Dr Trusler in 1799:

I feel that a Man may be happy in This World. And I know that This World is a World of Imagination & Vision. I see Everything I paint in This World, but Every body does not see alike. To the eyes of a Miser a Guinea is more beautiful than the Sun, & a bag worn with the use of Money has more beautiful proportions than a Vine filled with Grapes. The tree which moves some to tears of joy is in the Eyes of others only a Green thing that stands in the way. Some See Nature all Ridicule & Deformity, & by these I shall not regulate my proportions; & Some Scarce see Nature at all. But to the Eyes of the Man of Imagination, Nature is Imagination itself. As a man is, So he Sees, As the Eye is formed, such are its Powers.

You certainly Mistake, when you say that the Visions of Fancy are not to be found in This World. To Me This World is all One continued Vision of Fancy & Imagination.[5]

We may, perhaps unfairly, speculate that Dr Trusler would have been just the sort not to have expected our silence to have any intrinsic value – while we read that for Blake it was certainly an element of his visionary world. 'The moon like a flower/ In heaven's high bower,/ With silent delight/ Sits and smiles on the night.'[6]

The magnificent liturgy of the Eastern Orthodox churches represents a Christian development of this visionary approach to the highest point. The interior of their church buildings are often elaborately decorated. Almost every square inch of wall and ceiling surface may be covered with pictorial representations. Icons will also be on display and the iconostasis (a screen, covered with icons, separating nave from sanctuary) veils the celebration of the holy mysteries. The effect of this grand visual display is to transform the building from merely an enclosed space into being, as it were, a huge window on to spiritual realities. In entering the building one seems to move from the mundane world into the dimension of the communion of saints. The solemnity of the music, and the sophisticated symbolism of the ritual actions, all this conducted in a highly visual environment, serves to evoke a sense of the magisterial presence of God. To an unsympathetic observer this may seem very theatrical, but to the worshipper who enters fully into its meaning all thes elements of the liturgical celebration mediate God. They are outward and visible signs, highly stylized, but which become wholly transparent of an inward and spiritual grace. From the earliest days of the development of this great liturgical tradition, silence was used – as indeed it continues to be now. From the fifth-century 'Liturgical Homilies of Narsai' comes the following impressive description of a particular moment in the Eucharistic Prayer:

> ... all the ecclesiastical body now observes silence, and all set themselves to pray earnestly in their hearts. The Priests are still, and the deacons stand in silence ... the whole people is quiet and still, subdued and calm. ... The Mysteries are set in order, the censers are smoking, the lamps are shining. ... Deep silence and peaceful calm settles on that place.[7]

Anything less than silence at this particular moment would surely have detracted from the community's profound awareness of Divine presence. On the other hand, a friend once told me of an exploratory visit to a Quaker Meeting for Worship. He was totally baffled by the silence and spent the entire Meeting counting the panes of glass in the window facing him (there were 296 of them!). Sometimes in an act of worship we are aware only of mundane features. The signs point, but we do not see that to which they point. The Orthodox Liturgy may be capable of mediating a heavenly vision, but we are not in heaven yet! There may well be moments when silence evokes the breaking in of the extraordinary, but for most of us, for much of the time, our world is depressingly ordinary. We have indeed to take into account the fact that silence is often felt to be a commodity hard to handle in church worship.

It is indeed interesting to examine the place that silence usually has in current Anglican worship. We say it is important and we make some attempt to put this into practice. But at an average, 'middle-of-the-road', Parish Communion service it often does not seem at all easy to allow for natural periods of silence. Talking to other clergy makes me wonder whether we do not feel rather guilty about this. 'We *have* experimented with periods of silence, but have not persisted I'm afraid', 'There's just such a lot of material to get through in the hour, it's not easy to have long periods of silence' were typical comments from clergy. At the same time, one also occasionally hears comments from individual worshippers such as, 'Why can't Anglican clergy cope with more than the nominal twenty-second period of silence?' Silence in the liturgy does often seem to be handled rather clumsily. Frequently it will be introduced in a self-conscious manner – 'now we'll keep a time of silence in which we will think about ...' – and so many ideas are suggested that the silence is really not silence at all, but rather a period of much mental activity. So, we may feel silence is a desirable ingredient of worship, but we nevertheless often feel very ill at ease with it when it is allowed to occur. Why?

Silence is only mentioned once in the rubrics of the 1662 Book of Common Prayer, and that in the Ordering of Priests. No doubt Reformation liturgy was often greeted with the same complaint that sometimes meets its modern revision – 'all the mystery has gone out of the service!' The aim in both cases was to render Common Prayer more intelligible and so more accessible. One element that helped to give pre-Reformation worship the special depth that is perhaps referred to with the use of the word 'mystery' was silence. The entire Canon of the Mass, apart from two phrases, was said inaudibly by the priest. This was a practice that went back at least as far as the eighth century. After the Reformation, priest and people had to learn how to reinvest their new rationalized liturgy with the same depth. Silence was perhaps appreciated in different ways by different generations of churchgoers – though, sadly, scant specific evidence is left us. What we do know is that by Victorian times the 'early, quiet celebration' of Holy Communion was a well-established feature of Sunday worship. This service would have had a sense of intimate reverence and personal devotion distinct from the more robust heartiness of the later service of matins. Of course this sort of quietness occurred in a quite different way to that which was produced in the medieval Mass. The Victorians were happy with the quietness of their early service, just as pre-Reformation worshippers knew how to behave during the silent recitation of the Canon.

The fact is that with each new style of worship a new appreciation of silence has to be developed – in just the same way as new music and perhaps new internal decorations are also required. Those responsible for leading worship have to discover when and how to introduce silence into the service. This is not such a simple matter as it sounds. One has to be sensitive to the needs and conditions of particular congregations. Surely sometimes there *ought* to be a lot of chattering before the service begins? Some congregations will appreciate a long devotional silence after the Eucharistic thanks-giving prayer, while, for others, silence at the time of Intercession will be more important so as to allow spontaneous extemporary prayer. A lot of hard work needs to be done in the form of sensitive experimentation and thoughtful analysis before the right use of silence will be discovered. If this process is not conscientiously engaged in, however, the leaders of worship will never quite know how to use the silence, and the worshippers will never feel at ease with it. The more charitable conclusion is that we are at present still in the midst of the latest process of this sort. Many congregations have yet to discover the most appropriate form of silence for their worship.

A less charitable conclusion is that we have entered an era in which worship has been reduced to a superficial level. We go to church expecting to be entertained – with sing-along choruses or traditional nostalgic hymns, brief humorous sermons and a few nice prayers, all of which must have a topical slant and provide just enough spiritual reassurance. Silence is not particularly entertaining. Popular radio consists of an incessant flow of material, even the music is often 'voiced over'. No one sits looking at a blank television screen. Such media have conditioned us into expecting constant stimulation. Indeed, church worship, with the use of overhead projectors and electronic musical technology, often reaches high standards of entertainment. Mere silence, by contrast, can seem extraordinarily boring, unentertaining – and *deeply puzzling* to those who have been brought up with these expectations.

Here we reach a more fundamental explanation of our feeling very uneasy with silence in church – and it is what has already been said above. Silence is able to mediate a sense of the heavenly One – but we are not in heaven yet! Silence is not continuously sacramental, even for the most devout Christian. Although, to use Tillich's language, there are moments when silent contemplation becomes 'the bearer of a sacral power', these moments must perforce be set in the midst of long stretches of ordinariness. It simply has to be accepted that for most of the time silence will be non-eventful. A comparison may be made with our appreciation of the Eucharist. Just now and again the receiving of Holy Communion will be a fresh personal encounter with Christ. But for long periods, Sunday after Sunday, the sacrament seems empty of any personal meaning. We may well feel that we are going through the ritual in a mechanical way. What helps to keep us going, among other motives, is the memory of those times when the Eucharist *has* been deeply meaningful, when the breaking of bread has confronted us with Christ. Such moments cast an afterglow over the long stretches of non-eventfulness and sustain us. In the same way silence may mean nothing, but to those for whom it has once mediated a glimpse of the eternal, this nothingness can be accepted as a silence of waiting.

However, if silence has never worked in this way for a person they may wonder what it is they are supposed to be waiting for. Those of us who have developed a personal appreciation of silent contemplation have to remember that silence is a fundamentally mundane quality. It is only of interest because of what it may come to mediate. But sacraments do not work automatically. One has to be taught to appreciate them. Christians are only admitted to Holy Communion after a programme of catechesis. Similarly, an appreciation of silent contemplation has to be cultivated. Just how this can be encouraged will be discussed in the next chapter. But for those who have not developed a sacramental appreciation of silence, its imposition may seem a totally meaningless experience. If one Sunday the vicar suddenly announces an extended period of silence in the middle of the service, there may be a completely blank response from a confounded congregation. To some it will be like the child who has misbehaved at school and is made to stand facing the wall. As he stands there with his nose almost touching the wall, he wonders what to make of this bizarre non-experience. Similarly, the bemused congregation begin to feel rather silly and perhaps inadequate. What are they supposed to be doing? One remembers the Quaker attender who explained that he appreciated the weekly Meeting for Worship as an opportunity for planning the week's menus. At least he had the sense to make some practical use of what was, to him, an entirely neutral time of peace and quiet.

This helps us to understand why silence is clumsily handled, or even avoided altogether, in some contemporary worship. On a purely practical level, clergy and congregations have to think and experiment long and hard before they will discover the most appropriate use of silence for themselves. It does not come easily. And the desire for entertainment, if it is allowed to loom too large, will probably relegate silence as being too intense anyway. More seriously, an appreciation of silence has to be cultivated in the individual worshipper. A little simple instruction and guidance is an essential prerequisite. Even Quakers, who set such little store by 'notions', have their two-volume *Book of Discipline*, which teaches new members how to value and use the silent worship. But there is a yet more profound antipathy to silence that may be felt. Silence may be experienced as a non-event, lacking any meaning. If this is felt to be a neutral experience then one may simply have no interest in persisting with it. But silence may be more definitely negative if the non-meaning feels personally threatening and seems to put one in touch with very strong fears and anxieties.

To put it very crudely, man has slowly emerged as a thinking being and has become very aware of himself in distinction to the rest of the natural order. We feel we stand apart, set by virtue of our advanced development on a lonely pinnacle overlooking the rest of the world. The eighteenth-century period of the Enlightenment marks the most conscious phase of this process. The operation of

human reason assumed dominance and all traditional thought
structures were exposed to a critical spirit. The end result of this was
that the security of holding a particular 'world-view' was undermined as all beliefs were felt to have a relative value. To the
loneliness of a superior being was added a sense of alienation from
any absolute meaning. Modern existentialist thinkers have cate-
gorized this state of mind as the inherent condition of humanity.
They assert that we are estranged from our essential nature – which
we are to struggle to lay hold of in the future. Thus the present is
characterized by anxiety, loneliness, and a sense of estrangement. A
fear of chaos lurks beneath the surface – and can be quite terrifying.
The feeling that we are somehow 'lost' breeds a spiritual restlessness.

The existence of these feelings can be confirmed by reference to
much modern art and literature. The Norwegian artist Edvard
Munch (1863–1944) probed its depths.[8] In many of his paintings the
elements of loneliness and anxiety find expression. *The Dance of Life*
depicts the vitality and variety of life as couples dance together
representing physical desire. But in the corner stands a mournful
figure, starkly apart from the others, who looks on silently. In
another, *The Lonely Ones*, a man and a woman with their backs
turned look mutely out to sea. The mauves and browns convey a
sense of isolation and melancholy. But it is his painting *The
Scream*, perhaps the best known, which most dramatically
expresses the pain of this meaninglessness. The skull-like face,
mouth open, eyes round, is the focus of an agonized wail from all
alienated being. Munch described the experience that inspired this
painting: 'One evening I was walking along a path, the city on one
side, the fjord below. I felt tired and ill. . . . The sun was setting and
the clouds turning blood-red. I sensed a scream passing through
Nature; it seemed to me that I heard the scream. I painted this
picture, painted the clouds as actual blood. The colour shrieked.'

Now it is these deeply negative feelings that the keeping of silence
may unwittingly put us in touch with. Silence, it was said above,
connects easily with a sense of presence; it is an appropriate sign that
may then sacramentally mediate the holy presence of God. But
silence also connects easily with a sense of meaninglessness. It
reminds us of what are perhaps our deepest anxieties – the terror of
utter chaos, the fear that there *can* be no meaning, our fundamental
alienation from the possibility of ultimate fulfilment. It is no wonder
that in the practice of silent prayer one typically comes to the

point at which it seems profoundly repellent. The lack of meaning that liturgical silence has for some worshippers may not just be a neutral experience, it may indeed be deeply disturbing.

Such feelings may offer part of an explanation for the frenetic pace of modern life. We use our constant activity as a means to avoid contemplating the underlying meaninglessness. Perhaps, though, there is a more subtle and reciprocal link between our frenzied activism with its rapacious consumerism and our fear of chaos. The psychologist C. G. Jung wrote, 'Restlessness begets meaningless-ness, and the lack of meaning in life is a soul-sickness whose full extent and full import our age has not as yet begun to comprehend.'⁹ Perhaps, then, this begins to reveal the importance of silent contemplation in our angst-ridden age? It may be that the fear of chaos needs to be faced squarely and not continually evaded. The keeping of silence would certainly be an effective means for breaking through the vicious circle of restlessness which begets meaningless-ness which begets restlessness.

It must be accepted, then, that silence fully entered into will necessarily have an ambivalent, bitter-sweet quality. Silence is merely a mundane feature of our workaday world. We may not particularly seek it out – by, for example, deliberately waking in the middle of the night as some contemplative religious orders still do. But if we do we may discover that silence, ordinary as it is, has a particular power in alerting us to God's presence. It is the 'bearer of a sacral power', to use Tillich's language. But, while it is sometimes possible to interpret the datum of silence in this way, such moments of Divine disclosure will always be set in the midst of long stretches when the silence seems remorselessly dull and mundane. William Blake said that, 'The tree which moves some to tears of joy is in the Eyes of others only a thing which stands in the way.' But this is inevitable. Brief moments of sweetness have to sustain us through-out the bitterly long haul of our human pilgrimage to God. 'As they go through the thirsty valley they find water from a spring' (Ps. 84.6). More disturbingly, silence may also alert us to deep feelings of alienation and a profound fear of chaos. The highest moments of religious ecstasy cannot be separated from corresponding moments of human despair.

The Christian religious tradition (and, no doubt, other religious traditions) enables us to interpret silence in this way. We shall be exploring how this happens in the next chapter. But if the Church represents an arena in which such experience may occur, she must accept its bitter-sweet quality. Clergy and congregations may fight shy of silence in worship, and this is understandable if at times it represents non-meaning and even touches on some very raw nerves. However, to fill up all the liturgical spaces that might have remained silent is to deny one way in which worship is able to catch fire and become the vehicle for a vital encounter with God. It also makes the worship escapist in so far as the worshipping group are attempting to shield themselves from ordinariness and more particularly from their own possibly deep sense of alienation. The Church should surely be a place to *face*, not *flee* from, reality.

Christians are often very active people who conspicuously fail to practise the need for 'space' and prayer that is regularly preached. But there are certain practical ways in which we might hope to check the restless agitation that seems increasingly to mark our society. For example, the Christian contribution to the continuing debate about Sunday trading has tended to concentrate on the well-being of the family and the rights of shopworkers. But these important aspects should not be allowed to obscure the fact that for many of us Sunday is still a relatively *empty* day. Individuals may engage in sport and families go out in the car visiting, but it is still a day on which the majority are usually free to do what they choose. Perhaps this makes it a flat day in which people often feel at a loose end – and so wish they could relieve their boredom with some Sunday-afternoon shopping along a crowded High Street. Anything to escape the awful quietness of a traditional English Sunday? But our lives do not need filling with even more activity. It may be tempting always to overlay the ordinary with something entertaining that has more zest. But while this helps to keep the despair of human alienation well under the surface of our consciousness, its price is the negation of religious experience. This is the soul-sickness that Jung recognized.

First, of course, we must learn to practise ourselves what we preach. We have to cultivate an awareness of the *sacramental* significance of silence. The obvious model to aid the growth of this understanding is that sacrament with which we may well already be familiar, the Eucharist. If we have known what it is for the bread of Holy Communion both to represent the crucified and risen body of Christ, and to bring us to a real and personal encounter with him, then this same appraisal can be made of silence. The sacrament of the Eucharist and the sacramental potential of silence need to be placed side by side. The easiest way to do this is to find a church where the Blessed Sacrament is reserved. (This is done primarily for the purpose of taking Holy Communion to the sick and house-bound.) Make yourself comfortable and sit, or kneel, quietly. Think lovingly of those moments when Communion has brought you an influx of peace and joy – the very presence of Christ. Dwell too on the more frequent occasions when the service has seemed tiresome and devoid of meaning. Then stop and listen to the silence of the church. This too is a sign of God's very presence, and in the same sacramental way may bring you a personal intimation of that reality. Remember always that this sacramental silence will have a bitter-sweet quality, but that it is precisely in the painful emptiness of this desert that the spring of life can be found.

Notes

1 J. E. Bowers, 'Let the Lord's People', no. 146 in *More Hymns For Today*. Norwich, William Clowes & Sons, 1980.
2 H. Küng, *Does God Exist?* London, Collins, 1980, p. 551.
3 P. Tillich, lecture entitled 'Nature and Sacrament', in *The Protestant Era*. Chicago, University of Chicago Press, 1948, pp. 94–5.
4 I. Ramsey, *Religious Language*. London, SCM, 1957, p. 14.
5 W. Blake, *A Selection of Poems and Letters*, ed. J. Bronowski, Harmondsworth, Penguin, 1958, p. 220.
6 ibid., 'Night', p. 35.
7 C. Harris, 'Liturgical Silence', in *Liturgy and Worship*, ed. W. K. L. Clarke, London, SPCK, 1932, p. 779.
8 *The Dance of Life* and *The Scream* may be seen in the National Gallery in Oslo; *The Lonely Ones* at the Munch Museum, Oslo.
9 C. G. Jung, *The Structure of the Dynamics of the Psyche*. London, Routledge & Kegan Paul, 1960–9, p. 815.

3 · Rooting in Forgetfulness

Pocket calculators usually have a facility for storing figures in a 'memory', which can then be related to subsequent sums. This makes life much easier for those of us who find basic arithmetic hard enough, without also having to remember a whole string of numbers! Home computers have a yet more impressive memory, of course. Floppy discs are able to carry more words than we would expect even the most experienced actor to be able to remember. Most of us indeed are painfully aware of the inadequacy of our own memories. We forget important appointments and are regularly unable to remember names – sometimes, infuriatingly, even of people we know quite well. Similarly, we may feel that much of the material we once learnt in formal education has now, regrettably, been lost.

The reality, however, is that human intelligence has a prodigious capacity for remembering useful information. But the emphasis is on the word *useful*, for it is generally the information we need for day-to-day living that we remember most easily. Psychologists may speculate about the full range of our memory store cupboard, sometimes going so far as to suggest that in the deepest recesses of the mind we can even remember being in the womb. But what is more reliable is our ability to remember such things as where we live in relation to the maze of streets in our particular town; that we will be able to do our work, knowing that this form has to go there, and that certain procedure followed; that we can confidently read a thick book, and by page 450 still remember how the story was introduced on page 4. Our minds have many megabytes of information that are constantly being retrieved and applied. We really should not think so badly of our own memories! It is just that, for most of us, they have a rather practical bent.

In this sense we usually do not appreciate the full extent of our knowledge and understanding. It is only when we consider how easily we negotiate the tasks and problems of any ordinary day that we begin to realize just how much information has actually been used. We must not get confused here with the ability to exercise various skills, which is a rather different thing. I can ride a bicycle, but this did not involve the learning of any factual material. I simply managed a certain technique. On the other hand, when cycling out to the hospital where I am chaplain I ride consistently on the left-hand side of the road, I stop when I see an unbroken white line painted across the road in front of me, and I always extend my right hand when turning into the entrance. I learnt all this from a book – which was hard work at the time since I was young – but now I take the knowledge for granted and use it every day. Much of the factual information that we all possess, of so many different kinds, we are almost unconscious of. This is so because we are accustomed to *using* it – there is usually no need to think *about* it. Thus a large quantity of personally learnt material remains tacit, until, that is, we are induced for some reason to abstract it again from its pragmatic context.

The strongly empirical bias in modern thought has already been noted, but in this chapter we must seriously ask whether things are really as simple and straightforward as is implied. Again I ask for the reader's patience as we pursue this question. Although the matter may seem to become a bit dry and academic, we will in fact be securing an understanding fundamental to the appreciation of silence as the way to an encounter with God. Representatives of empiricism have wanted to stress the importance of our physical sense impressions. John Locke (1632–1704), the British founding father of this school, claimed that the material objects of our experience consist of primary and secondary qualities.[1] The primary qualities are those of 'solidity, extension, figure, motion or rest, and number', and these represent the actual qualities of the object itself. Through our sense impressions of these qualities we are able to have reliable experience of the object. He admits that our experience of the secondary qualities, such as sounds, colours, smells, and tastes, are not 'in' the object itself. But even these, he says, are to do with the 'powers' of the object. The exact details of the way in which Locke understood the relationship between observer and object are complex and rather confusing. But the main thrust of his work was the assertion that to know the real world we must simply open our eyes (and the other senses) and take account of that experience. Most of what we know comes directly through our physical senses. 'Let us then suppose the mind to be, as we say, white paper, void of all characters, without any ideas; how comes it to be furnished?... To this I answer in one word, from experience: in that all our knowledge is founded, and from that it ultimately derives itself.' Certainly Locke agreed that we derive some ideas from our own ratiocinations (which he understood as an internal observation of our own minds), but he still insisted that all our ideas fundamentally originate from sensory impressions: 'the first step and degree towards knowledge, and the inlet of all the materials of it'.

To read this you would think the nature of the material world to be fairly self-evident, to know which we simply need to train ourselves to be careful observers. Indeed, this is what many empirical thinkers have said, with varying degrees of emphasis on the directness of the passage of data from object to observer. Bertrand Russell pointed to (at least some) experiences as being precisely of this kind.[2] If, for example, you slip on a piece of orange peel and bang your head on the pavement, there will simply be *no doubt* about your resulting experience. So there are 'some occurrences that I cannot make myself doubt', and he concluded that much of our experience has an immediacy and a reliability in this manner. But if experience is so simple, then what function does that information stored away secretly in our minds have, for much of it would seem to be in constant, if tacit, *use?* It may be that ideas do originate from experience, but should we not say that ideas also play a vital role when we have experience?

William Blake commented that a tree 'moves some to tears of joy', while for others it is only 'a green thing that stands in the way'. [3] But, whether we have a poetic soul or not, the recognition of an object in our path as 'a tree' requires a particular interpretation of data. When I recognize a patch of green as leaves and a rough texture as bark I am drawing upon certain understandings that I possess. I understand that the world consists of other objects as well as myself. I expect a particular type of tree to have a certain definite shape. I know that a tree has roots that extend deep into the ground, and ensure that it is unlikely to fall on me. I have learnt that leaves turn brown in autumn and are shed in winter. These ideas, and doubtless many others, come into play when I experience 'a tree'. The actual nature of the tree is not self-evident. There are raw data; my sense impressions provide me with these. But these physical sensations have to be interpreted before I can really *experience the tree*.

So I agree with those who argue that empirical thinkers have overstated their case by stressing the priority of pure observation. The objection is that strict empiricists have failed to appreciate fully that the observer comes to his task fairly bristling with ideas and theories and, most importantly, that he *needs* them for the work. Yet in one sense these enthusiasts for empiricism might be forgiven. The level at which these theories are used is hidden, and their very existence is easily forgotten. Indeed we interpret data most efficiently when theory is used unconsciously. When the craftsman begins to notice the tool he is using, the quality of the artefact usually suffers. Michael Polanyi has in recent years contributed a seminal exploration of this theme, which he named 'the tacit dimension'.[4] He confirms the view that our experience consists of data and interpretation together, 'the act of knowing includes an appraisal'. He coined the phrase 'personal co-efficient' to refer to the act of appraisal that experience *always* includes (whether we realize it or not): 'this personal co-efficient . . . shapes all factual knowledge'. Most important, he stresses that it is as if we 'live in' those particular theories that we use to experience the world: 'personal knowledge . . . commits us, passionately and far beyond our comprehension, to a vision of reality. . . . For we live in it as in the garment of our own skin.'

This important lesson about the way in which we experience the material world helps to explain the nature of religious experience too. Earlier I imagined a particular encounter with silence. 'A person enters an empty church one sunny afternoon and finds it a peaceful place to sit for a few moments and relax. But the silence impels another person, who enters later, to slip to her knees with a sudden sense of awe.' I then asked what it was that would make two people interpret the same phenomenon in different ways. My answer was that it would be to do with 'the beliefs, the values and the expectations that they bring to the experience'. I would not expect the individuals to be aware of this mental equipment with which the silence is interpreted. The latter person experienced a sense of awe. The experience consisted of data and interpretation, silence and personal religious beliefs – but the beliefs remained tacit. However, without those particular beliefs it could not have been a *religious* experience, as indeed it was not for the first person.

Silence has the power of mediating the presence of God, in the same sacramental way as the Eucharistic bread and wine have the power to mediate an involvement in the death and resurrection of

Christ. Those who participate in any sacrament have to be initiated into its mysteries. That is, the meaning of the symbol has to be clearly explained and related to that which is being celebrated. Those who find silence deeply significant in a religious sense show that the necessary theoretical spade work has been done. At some stage they have learnt their Christian 'catechism', basic doctrines have been read, marked, learnt – and then inwardly digested. This final assimilation of the ideas learnt is important, for it enables a quick and effective application of them in the act of interpretation. The second person coming into the silent church unconsciously draws upon, for example, her faith in the reality of God, her trust that God loves her in a personal way, her understanding that God is able to be extremely close to her in an invisible but spiritual way, and perhaps a particular biblical text such as 'our God is a consuming fire' (Heb. 12.29). All these elements explain why she responds to the silence with a sense of awe. Certainly she would be able to articulate them, and does so in times of discussion with others. But at the moment these ideas and beliefs are being used, and for this reason remain tacit. To think about them would be disastrous, as with the cyclist who rides into a lamp-post when he begins consciously to rehearse the rules of the Highway Code in his mind!

In a way, it hardly seems necessary to attempt to justify the assertion that ideas, including religious beliefs, have most value when they are applied. We respect those who merely think, but those whose thinking has benefited mankind in some practical way are most rewarded. Certainly there is a need for the pure theoretician, in theology as in other spheres of human activity, but an unapplied concept, however brilliantly conceived, cries out for physical actualization. George Bernard Shaw's quip bites home: 'He who can, does. He who cannot, teaches'. Actual experience of God is of infinitely greater value than thoughts *about* God, however sophisticated the latter and crude the former. The logical progression of religious thoughts is to feed experience – there can be no experience without the wherewithal to interpret the data.

It is also easy to see that ideas are most effectively applied when the practitioner has become very accustomed to handling them – when they are old friends, tried and tested. The first few times a new understanding is applied, the result is clumsy and self-conscious. It is much easier when the ideas in use become, as it were, second nature. This is exactly how it is with religious experience. You may be able to remember how it felt when you first learnt to pray. You laboured away at it, more aware of the mechanics of the prayer than of the praying itself. Eventually the new concepts you were struggling to apply disappeared from view and you were fully embarked on a growing prayerful relationship with God.

Much of the contents of our minds, learnt originally in an abstract form, have been metamorphosed into a pragmatic, functional form. The manner in which we digest food is a useful metaphor with which to describe this process (though there is, as I shall take pains to explain later, one important difference!). Just as we may be served with an appetizing plate of nutritious food, so our religious teachers attempt to feed our spiritual formation with the wholesome doctrines of the Christian faith. But however enjoyable the meal, when skilfully cooked, the main point of the exercise is to nourish the body. The vegetables will be turned into energy. Similarly, the aim of spiritual teaching is not merely to furnish the mind with orthodox beliefs, but to prompt a personal encounter with God. Beliefs are to be digested into a pragmatic form.

The question may now arise, 'How do I digest my religious beliefs?' But, to continue the metaphor, it is as complex and as unnecessary to provide this amount of explanation as it is to explain in detail to a child precisely how food is digested and turned into energy. All you need to know is to open your mouth when the meal is served, to handle the fork, chew, swallow – and then to get on with living energetically. The physical process of the digestion of food occurs quite naturally and does not require our conscious awareness. The body is already attuned to a pragmatic function. In exactly the same way, I believe it is utterly natural for us to experience the presence of God. So long as we are fed an adequate supply of spiritual nourishment this will automatically be digested into the form that will facilitate a personal sense of God. Unfortunately, while we all learn to eat at a tender age, in our a-religious culture the automatic ability to obtain spiritual nourishment is often unnaturally neglected. We need reminding of this basic 'digestive' function that we all possess, and so at the end of this chapter one particular method, that of '*lectio divina*', will be described.

We have now proceeded a little further with our account of what happens when silence is appreciated as a sacramental experience of the presence of God. There is the absence of sound and activity. This state is interpreted by certain religious beliefs. These beliefs have

been so digested as to have become the accustomed mode of being
for that individual. They characterize his world-view of meaningful
activity. The beliefs are hidden or tacit in so far as they have come to
have a pragmatic significance. But look, a common feature of
Christian mysticism is the claim that the essential experience is itself
beyond words. It is understood as a glimpse of the Divine other-
worldly which mortal minds are naturally incapable of grasping
fully, and which this-worldly language is logically inadequate to
express. In his book on the English mystics, Dom David Knowles
explained their central experience in exactly these terms: '[it] is
wholly incommunicable, save as a bare statement, and in this respect
all the utterances of the mystics are entirely inadequate as
representations of the mystical experience, but it brings absolute
certainty to the mind of the recipient'.[5]

The ineffable nature of profound religious experience has itself
thus classically been taken as a mark of authentication. Knowles
magisterially surveys the history of Christian mysticism, watered
from the springs of neo-Platonism, and humbly imbibes the simple
truth of this feature of the experience. Early on, it achieved
definitive status in the writings honorifically ascribed to the
Dionysius mentioned in the Acts of the Apostles. The 'Mystical
Theology'[6] begins with the following explicit appeal: 'practise
intensely the mystic contemplations and leave behind the senses, and
the intellectual activities, all sensible and intelligible things, . . . and
raise yourself to union, in ignorance with him who is above all being
and knowledge'.

One very useful effect of this claim is to provide for an ultimate
defence of the validity of mystical experience against all opponents.
Whatever they may say, the only person truly able to judge the
experience is the one who has had it – and, says the mystic, once one
has had such an experience, no shred of doubt will remain. Of
course, to any opponents this may well represent the ultimate self-
deception. And it should not, I believe, be taken at face value. In
fact, the emphasis on ineffability (and, as in Pseudo-Dionysius, it is
often stressed very heavily) actually helps to confirm the understanding we have now reached of the *tacit* role of beliefs in silent
encounter with God.

The writings ascribed to Dionysius assume that God is the reality
from whom we, as created beings, proceed. By virtue of this
creaturely relationship with the Creator, we are able to attain to some

sort of knowledge of him. But it is also stressed that God, strictly speaking, is quite beyond the range of human reason. We are only able to know him in terms of his outgoing response of love, an ecstasy in which our limited beings are taken up into God's Being. Of this encounter there is properly nothing we can say. Indeed, the writings refer to a meeting with God 'in unknowing'. Now this would seem to be a clear denial of our approach. I have said that we need our beliefs to interpret the data of experience. But Pseudo-Dionysius has said that human conceptions of God must, in their inadequacy, be denied. I have said that we must digest and enter into the meaning of our beliefs, but Pseudo-Dionysius implies that we must abandon our attempts to fathom out God and let ourselves be taken up by him. For him, the encounter with God must be, literally, ineffable.

Certainly these writings ascribed to Dionysius make a valuable corrective in the history of Christian spirituality. We *should* be wary of the limited nature of human ideas when applied to God himself. But in dealing with personal experience, the same error exists as is made by those who take empiricism too far. It is the implication that some data can be meaningful without the need for any interpretation on the part of the one who experiences. The writings of Pseudo-Dionysius, and indeed the writings of so many mystics (St John of the Cross, the author of *The Cloud of Unknowing*, and the twentieth-century Evelyn Underhill, for example), imply that if we consciously reject our own personal ideas about God we will be left with a pure experience of God himself. This is a false assumption. Data, even data of God, may be present and may impinge upon us, but they will be absolutely without meaning until we are able to interpret them. To literally reject human concepts of God is to bar the way to personal experience of him.

Steven Katz, in a highly influential contribution to the book *Mysticism and Philosophical Analysis*,[7] establishes an important principle which I think we must accept. This is that the key to understanding religious experience is the beliefs that are held, because our beliefs shape our experience: 'these images, beliefs, symbols and rituals define in advance what the experience [the mystic] wants to have, and which he then does have, will be like'.

Now this may sound rather harsh and overly deterministic. Many liberal-minded Christians like to feel that the main world religions generate a common experience of the Ultimate. But, while there is undoubtedly some experiential overlap, to assume that we all experience the same thing is to imply that we all share the same beliefs – which is patently not so. Katz is right to draw attention to some of the stark contrasts that exist between religions, in belief and consequently in experience too. For example, he explains:

> One is especially struck in Jewish mysticism by the imagery of love, even including very pronounced sexual imagery which is used to express all sorts of 'relations' relevant to the kabbalistic mind. This aspect is totally absent from early Indian Buddhism which equates sexuality with desire and sees desire as the basic element which causes suffering, and which is to be overcome in nirvana.

It is perhaps significant that religious people of divergent traditions are sometimes relatively unaware of the differences between them. This may be attributable to the covert mode of beliefs when employed in the interpretation of experience. We tend to overlook our beliefs in our enthusiasm for experience. But, however tacit they are, experience necessarily presupposes the existence and use of beliefs.

The writings accorded to Dionysius will be misleading if the advice to raise oneself to a state of holy 'ignorance' is taken literally. However, while we may feel out of tune with the neo-Platonic vision of reality that underlies such language, it may yet provide us with some contemporary spiritual nourishment. After all, this teaching is not merely a piece of speculative philosophizing, but must surely represent the fruits of a disciplined perseverance in prayer on the part of one very sincere individual. When we are told to 'leave behind ... intellectual activities', we may read this as the need to leave off self-conscious intellectual ratiocination about God. There comes a time when progress will only be made if a person moves on from personal speculation *about* God into a present and immediate *encounter* with him. Strictly speaking, this has been the traditional distinction between 'meditation' and 'contemplation'. *The Cloud of Unknowing*,[8] written probably by a fourteenth-century English parish priest, describes meditation in the following way: 'an awareness of one's own wretched state, sorrow and contrition, a sympathetic and understanding consideration of Christ's passion and that of his servants, a gratitude which praises God for his wonderful gifts, his kindness and works in all parts of his creation, physical and spiritual'.

This is a detached stance, an evaluation of our Christian beliefs and an analysis of how we thereby stand with God. It may be imagined as our drawing the map of religious belief – while contemplation is to take this map and boldly step out into the unknown: 'contemplation – at least as we know it in this life – is wholly caught up in darkness, and in this cloud of unknowing, an outreaching love and a blind groping for the naked being of God, himself and him only'.

But the point is that it would be foolish literally to leave behind the map. It is the art of cartography that must be left behind as one now concentrates on the journey itself. The traveller uses the map, indeed his safety may depend upon it. But it is no longer the map itself, rather the place it guides him to, that is now the focus of attention. The theory is applied and becomes useful. This is exactly what the author of Dionysius' writings urges us to do. We must leave behind the detached consideration of beliefs and learn to apply them. We must use them in the interpretation of data, and so be led to a personal encounter with him of whom they first taught us.

Pseudo-Dionysius tells us to aim at a state of 'ignorance with him who is above all being and knowledge'. Now of course this says something about the Divine object of our experience himself; namely, that whatever we know of God there is always more to be known. This is another reason for our silence before God, and it is a theme that we must take up later. But it also says something about the status of beliefs once we have left behind the meditation of them and begun to use them in the contemplation of God. We are then no longer aware of the beliefs in themselves. Through application they have become tacit. In this digested form they most effectively feed and sustain our continuing experience of God. The word 'ignorance' is therefore a quite proper description of our state, but it has a strictly relative meaning. The cyclist not thinking 'about' the Highway Code can be said at that moment to be ignorant of it. But in so far as he unconsciously rode according to its directions, he would show that he had learnt and digested its meaning. However, we must also remember that, if need be, he would be *able* to stop, dismount and articulate this knowledge for the benefit, say, of an interrogating policeman. But in the contemplative encounter itself we are in a sense ignorant of God, for we are not thinking 'about' him.

The distinction between meditation and contemplation is a subtle one and perhaps rather confusing. There certainly is a shift of gear between the objective consideration of beliefs and the believing encounter with God, not as a once-for-all demarcation, however, but rather as a continuous mutual interplay between the two. We need to allow ourselves periods of time, a personal space, in which we simply aim to be reflective. We should use these opportunities to mull over our beliefs quietly – and it may be that in the silence of such reflection a personal apprehension of God will dawn on us. At one moment we may be meditating on our convictions picturing a biblical scene perhaps, or working through a logical argument. This will represent the process of mental digestion, allowing us to distil the essence of its meaning. But then the next moment may bear us into a personal disclosure of God, and what will have happened is that the pragmatic interpretative potential of those beliefs has suddenly been realized.

You see, in the work of contemplation, silence represents both the datum to be interpreted and the assimilation of those beliefs that will be used to make the interpretation. The beliefs are silent in the sense that they are now tacit. The datum is silence, which we come to appreciate as a sacrament of the presence of God. Both stages may be described as an act of reflection. When engaged in quiet spiritual reflection it becomes quite difficult to separate the different forms and functions of silence in operation. A peaceful place away from noise and chatter will probably be chosen for this sort of prayer, and the prayer itself may induce a sense of inner stillness. This outward and inner stillness necessary for concentrating on our beliefs itself becomes the data to be interpreted and then finally the actual medium of experience. Fortunately, in practice there is no particular need to separate these silences, but just to get silently on with the work in hand. The priority to be observed is for Christians to be reflective.

This priority is to be placed as a challenge before each of us. In Western European society we are all guilty of the obsessive desire to over-achieve. Does there not seem to be a common feeling that the meaning of life is to achieve as much as possible? Certainly this rubs off on our Churches, which all have long agendas of business. It might sound horribly complacent to suggest that we should all sit back and contemplate more, and act less. The biblical world-weariness of Ecclesiastes is, however, a salutary reminder of the ultimate sense of emptiness that rewards those who act first and ponder second:

Vanity of vanities, says the preacher, vanity of vanities! All is vanity. What does man gain by all the toil at which he toils under the sun?

All the toil of man is for his mouth, yet his appetite is not satisfied.

Who is like the wise man? And who knows the interpretation of a thing? A man's wisdom makes his faces shine, and the hardness of his countenance is changed (Eccles. 1.2–3; 6.7; 8.1).

A continual restlessness is also endemic in our day. Governments aspire to ever-higher standards of national prosperity. Individuals find contentment elusive, as indicated for example by the fragility of marriage relationships. We are never satisfied. Like tired restless children we often feel that we do not really know what it is that we want. The easy availability and widespread use (and abuse) of credit cards is another symptom of our malaise, revealing the desire for immediate results.

Some view the brash and brittle quality of our society as similar to the burn-out that heralded the final demise of the Roman Empire. Such generalized comparisons have a certain appeal, but cannot do justice to the complexity of a world in which societies are now so clearly interdependent. But what this condition does do is to throw into even greater relief the priority of spiritual reflection. God is indeed the ground of our being, and the rootlessness and lack of meaning that so many currently feel can only be transcended through the renewal of a sense of communion with him. The enigmatic words that Jesus speaks to Martha in Luke's Gospel speak to us of the need to penetrate through the superficial by way of cultivating a reflective spirit. Mystical experience needs rescuing from being thought of as an esoteric practice for a monastic elite. The priority of reflection is a universal appeal. 'Martha, Martha, you are anxious and troubled about many things; one thing is needful. Mary has chosen the good portion, which shall not be taken away from her' (Luke 10.41–42).

We should, however, beware of expecting silent reflection to be merely a cosily pious activity. Pondering deeply our beliefs and convictions is certainly the way for us to assimilate their essential meaning and make them fruitful of personal experience. But, if seriously engaged in, the silence may also prompt a radical questioning of those beliefs. Indeed, the process of assimilation, far from subduing our critical faculties, actually requires a rigorous sifting of what seems to us true from what seems to be false. Only so can we arrive at a view of reality to which we are firmly committed – which we are able to 'live in', as Polanyi says, 'as in the garment of our own skin'. So as we quietly sit and think about our beliefs, sucking out the nourishment from them and applying them to the very same silence of that which marks our concentration, the silence may suddenly turn into an affront. For this space we have created for thought will allow us to recognize objections to our beliefs; it will grant us the opportunity to develop an alternative view until it becomes impossible to evade the question mark any longer. The work of pondering, patiently pursued, may begin to reveal to us the cracks in the edifice of our spiritual vision. The sense of an internal incoherence, successfully glossed over and elaborated away in the affirmative verbalizing of belief, may in silence be painfully exposed. In our reflective silence we may actually begin to hear other voices than that of our own beloved religious tradition – that is, the voices of those who want to tell the other side of the story. And, since the function of silence is to encourage our readiness to listen, listen we must, however uncomfortable this may make us feel.

It is a mark of spiritual weakness and immaturity when we imagine the radical questioning of belief to be confined to academic theologians, while for the deepening of our prayer we turn for help to more traditionally-minded spiritual gurus. In the sort of reflective silence that we have been considering in this chapter, the two belong inseparably together. We should be careful to avoid the type of spirituality that is merely consoling and advertises as its aims the achievement of 'peace' and 'wholeness'. A good example of the latter might be thought to be the modern practice of Transcendental Meditation (TM) – except that it claims to be a-religious. In an article in The *Sunday Times Magazine* in December 1988, the journalist John Harding described what TM had done for him:

It was a Saturday. A fine day; the sun was shining, the birds were singing. I was floating across Eaton Square, my feet barely touching the ground. And I had arrived at this state simply by sitting in a chair doing next to nothing. It lasted all day. Normally a reluctant shopper, I dazzled my girlfriend with my willingness to browse and buy. I positively enjoyed driving through West End traffic, opening doors for others, giving way to them in queues and apologising when they trod on my toes.

Harding went on to explain in more detail for the reader what he actually did while 'sitting in a chair doing next to nothing':

> It entails sitting quietly with eyes closed for 20 minutes twice a day, and mentally repeating a single word or 'mantra'. . . . During meditation I am aware that I am in an altered state of consciousness quite unlike anything else. It is blissful. Breathing becomes shallow and slows along with the metabolism.

Now there are certainly some points of similarity between this account of TM and the practice of Christian contemplation. Perhaps this is why Christians have sometimes been so defensively antagonistic towards the Maharishi's organization? It professes to involve no religious belief (though adherents go through an initiation ceremony involving flowers, fruit, etc. in a semi-darkened room, with a picture of a guru on a sort of an altar, and one wonders if it is not really a variety of Hinduism dressed up for Western consumption), and yet promises to deliver the goods of religion – peace, happiness and well being! We may judge that TM is essentially a technique of relaxation, bodily, mental and in a sense spiritual too. On this level it must be acknowledged that relaxation has been, and is, commonly taught as a necessary preparation for Christian contemplation. The fundamental difference between TM and our reflective silence is that the latter is a rigorous committment to reality, and therefore so much more than a means for a quick and easy 'peace'. Harding told us, 'The euphoria of my first week soon levelled out, but since that time I have not for one moment felt depressed, nor have I suffered negative thoughts.' Reflective silence leads us to confront, and expressly *not* to evade, negative thoughts.

When we say, then, that contemplative silence is a sacrament of the presence of God, we have to acknowledge that the path towards this encounter will be profoundly challenging. The very same reflection that encourages the assimilation of our beliefs will prompt a tough questioning of them. Thus we may find ourselves caught in a painful dilemma. On the one hand, we possess certain religious convictions that we have felt drawn to reflect upon and enter into more deeply. On the other hand, the act of reflection inevitably opens up a space in which our points of certainty are open to attack.

TM calms, soothes and helps to bring us into harmony with the more positive and creative aspects of our personality. The mantra provides us with a security object to grab when we begin to feel vulnerable again. Perhaps, in reality, much Christian prayer is like this. But a merely affirmative prayer will not bring us to God. If we are fully open to a reflective silence we will need to affirm and to question, to think we know and then realize that we do not know. It is to accept a state of ambiguity in which there will be a faint echo of Christ's cry from out of the silence of Calvary – the knowledge of 'My God, my God', and its questioning 'Why hast thou forsaken me?' TM, and all merely consoling spirituality, seeks to avoid such disturbing questioning.

Nature abhors a vacuum and the Christian abhors ambiguity – religion, after all, is the attempt to be grounded in ultimate certainties. Reflective silence provides for a rejuvenating experience of God which is no less than an encounter with the 'Rock of our Salvation' (Ps. 95.1). But this is a certainty not of our own making. If we wish to be rooted in God – rather than merely lulled by the half-truths of our necessarily inadequate human beliefs – then we must plunge bravely into that reflective silence where ambiguity has to be faced. Perhaps a greater familiarity with this type of reflective prayer would help the Church of our day to handle some critical issues. For example, at the present time the Church of England finds itself heir to two separate movements – the movement for the ordination of women, and the ecumenical movement for the reconciliation of all Christian Churches. These are both liberal movements and, while they each have a separate history, it is often the same individuals who are most deeply committed to both goals. Many parts of the Anglican communion have now ordained women as priests, and there is a bright light at the end of the legislative tunnel for Church of England proponents. At the same time, the Anglican/ Roman Catholic International Commission has successfully covered much of the ground which, with official consensus, could open the way for the restoration of full communion. The Pope has, however, clearly articulated the view that when Anglicans ordain women they choose to shelve these ecumenical prospects. Those individuals who combine support for both movements now find themselves in a position of ambiguity.

Perhaps for many the ambiguity is eased by the demands of more practical matters, such as the need for more clergy and the strength of pressure groups. Others may sense the weakness of choosing to take the line of least resistance, and opt instead to remain with their sense of ambiguity. This will be a familiar situation for those who practise our reflective silence. When silently mulling over one's beliefs, one becomes aware of objections and inconsistencies. One may even feel that to permit the conflict to continue is ultimately to accept a degree of self-destruction, and no less than this may indeed be the price we have to pay. A spirituality that merely affirms our own prejudices, however venerable, must finally be self-defeating. It is to cling to an appreciation that is not of God, but is of ourselves. To pray contemplatively is to enter deeply into the traditions of the Christian faith, yes, and to bring them to life in our own experience of God. But the prerequisite for that Divine encounter is our willingness to have those cherished beliefs questioned, and perhaps for them to be sacrificed. Only so will we come to that certainty that is not of our own making. Inevitably, this current crisis will be handled by negotiation with expediency ruling the day. One wonders how different the outcome would be if, instead, our concerns were immersed long and deep in the uncompromising silence of reflection.

In the history of Christian spirituality, various methods by which to pursue a reflective consideration and assimilation of beliefs have been contrived. Few are as simple, direct and effective as that known in medieval monasticism as *lectio divina*. This is the reading of Scripture (or some other religious text) on one's own in a meditative way. The sense of the passage is deeply pondered upon and turned into prayer. The practice of *lectio divina* is traditionally associated with that fifth-century pioneer of biblical scholarship, St Jerome. The Latin Vulgate translation of the Bible is his great monument, for Jerome applied to this work his belief in the need to understand the original languages of the Scriptures. Furthermore, while others delighted in discovering allegorical meanings, Jerome directed more attention to the literal meaning of the text. Nevertheless, Jerome too stressed that the Bible should be studied prayerfully, for therein one would receive heavenly nourishment. He spoke of a 'Table of the Word' standing alongside the 'Table of the Sacrament'. In many of his letters Jerome recommended to his correspondents the value of reflective reading of Scripture as itself a form of prayer. In this he was drawing upon a well-established Christian approach to the Bible. St Cyprian wrote shortly after his conversion in the third century to his friend Donatus: 'Prayer in reading should be your constant concern; you speak with God and God then speaks with you.'

Cyprian indicates here how *lectio divina* is itself a particular method of engaging in that mutuality that characterizes silent reflection – the content of our faith is deeply assimilated and we are ourselves questioned in the silence of that process. The fifth-century monk John Cassian describes this spiritual interaction even more clearly in his *Conferences*.[9] (These recount his conversation with the principal exponents of Eastern monasticism.) On the one hand, he said that we are to appropriate the meaning of Scripture so as to enrich our understanding: 'Somehow the beauty of it [Scripture] stands out more and more as we get farther into it. Scripture shapes itself to human capacity.' But on the other hand, we must expect our previous understanding to be challenged and changed through this encounter with the Bible. 'Having banished all worldly concerns and thoughts, strive in every way to devote yourself constantly to the sacred reading so that continuous meditation will seep into your soul and, as it were, will shape it to its image.'

Lectio divina is an easily accessible form of prayer for us today. Having found a time and a place in which we can be quiet and relatively free from outward distractions, we shall need first to induce in ourselves a prayerful state of mind. Some such phrase as 'Lord, open me to your word' may suffice, followed by a pause to relax the body and calm the mind. Then we can begin our reading, and the Gospels will perhaps both be most enriching and most challenging. As we work through the text, sooner or later a particular word or phrase will strike us as having a personal meaning. This is the time to stop reading and to pursue the meaning that it has for us. We must feel free to ponder this for as long as it is fruitful, and only return to the text when we have exhausted its meaning. It will not matter if we read only three words at one sitting. We shall only be able to digest a certain amount in one go, and we must be careful not to overload the silence of our reflection. The patient practice of *lectio divina* will come to enrich our minds with a thoroughly assimilated range of spiritual meaning – and this tacit material can be applied as we discover God's presence in the silence.

A contemporary theologian, John Macquarrie, has expressed very eloquently the total honesty that theological reflection requires.[10]

His words apply just as much to ordinary believers as they patiently mull over their beliefs:

> We talk of scholars being 'devoted' to their subject and of the 'rigour' and 'strictness' of their pursuit of the truth. Thinkers in all subjects have also to learn the meaning of *metanoia* or change of mind and repentance, when their studies lead them to set aside long cherished theories and opinions in the light of fuller truth. Perhaps this is especially painful in theology, which is in fact inseparable from a kind of mystification. Everything in one's mind, no matter how long or how tenaciously one has clung to it, must be brought into the light, tested and scrutinized, and, if it stands in the way of fuller truth, be allowed to die. This is painful, for something of oneself dies with it.

A true *devotion* to Christian beliefs is precisely what *lectio divina* helps us to cultivate as we, so to speak, make them our own. Beliefs that we fail to appropriate will be of no use in facilitating that living encounter with God – and this must surely be the mainspring of our religion. So Macquarrie strikes the right chord when he says that 'the heart of theology is deep meditation on the great central themes of Christian faith'. Study and active thought has to be turned into prayer. 'The mind has to be open and receptive to the themes which it entertains.' In the personal space that reflection creates, our thoughts will reverberate freely and our minds will wrestle and be wrestled with. Slowly, as the bee patiently sucks nectar, we will learn to interpret the whole of this engagement with silence as encounter with God.

Notes

1 See J. Locke, *An Essay Concerning Human Understanding*, ed. and, abbrev. A. D. Woozley, London, Fontana, 1964, book II, ch.1, sec.2.
2 B. Russell, *Human Knowledge, Its Scope and Limits*. London, George Allen & Unwin, 1948, p. 188.
3 A letter to the Reverend Dr Trusler, August 1799, in W. Blake, *A Selection of Poems and Letters*, ed. J. Bronowski, Harmondsworth, Penguin, 1958, p. 220.
4 M. Polanyi, *Personal Knowledge*. London, Routledge & Kegan Paul, 1958, pp. 15–16.
5 D. Knowles, *The English Mystical Tradition*. London, Burns & Oates, 1961, p. 2.
6 Dionysius the Areopagite, *On the Divine Names and The Mystical Theology*, trans. C.E. Rolt, London, SPCK, 1957, I.1.

7 S. Katz, ed., *Mysticism and Philosophical Analysis*. London, Sheldon Press, 1978, p. 40.
8 C. Wolters, trans., *The Cloud of Unknowing*. Harmondsworth, Penguin, 1961, p. 63.
9 J. Cassian, *Conferences*, Classics of Western Spirituality. London, SPCK, 1985, p. 164–5.
10 'Prayer and Theological Reflection', in C. Jones, G. Wainwright, and E. Yarnold, eds, *The Study of Spirituality* (London, SPCK, 1986), p. 586.

4 · *To Wait*

There is a danger that we might make a fetish out of silence if we seek it rather *too* self-consciously. We should beware of this in our modest attempt to redress the relative imbalance in, what can become, 'poor talkative little Christianity'. What is being recommended here is indeed a more contemplative, reflective form of Christian life in which the option of silent prayer moves into a more central position. But I wish to emphasize the *natural* presence of silence throughout all human experience. Western European urban consumerism may be highly successful at evading it, but my point is that plain ordinary silence represents a potential for human growth that we are the poorer for denying. In coming to appreciate this, we will find that we have dug into a rich seam. There are just so many different kinds of silence. Perhaps this simply represents the sparkling, multi-faceted character of our relationship with the Divine. Some kinds of silence are deeply refreshing and immediately therapeutic – as in the daily meditations of those who practise TM. But we have already begun to see that silence is often profoundly disturbing. Those who choose a thoroughly active life perhaps realize that there is much in quiescence better kept well at bay. Silence provokes a radical questioning of beliefs that have previously granted a sense of security. It allows inner forces of chaos, angst and alienation to rear their heads. To permit silence is deliberately to make ourselves vulnerable.

We come now to consider that resigned, patient silence of waiting. Why *do* we find it so hard to wait for things? Are we all generally less patient these days, as was suggested in the last chapter? The queues for consumer goods are a notorious feature of Soviet life, and we may pity those who have to stand and wait for their daily bread. But are not we the ones to be pitied, with our chronic inability to wait for anything? A recent directive from the management of a large supermarket chain in Britain stated that check-out operators must be trained to handle twenty-two items per minute. This prompted a letter to *The Independent*, in which it was asked, tongue in cheek, 'whether we [the customers] may also have the benefit of a training video showing how to sort, pack and load these items at an approximately similar rate!'. This forms an amusing, if trivial, illustration of the high value we often place on a speedy delivery of the goods (whatever they are) – and then of our consequent feeling that life is just too fast to be coped with, which is a reaction to it. If we are in a positive frame of mind, then, we may attribute our contemporary impatience to a common sense of the huge potential for economic, social and technological growth. Chiming in with more personal hopes for emotional fulfilment, and the enjoyment of ever-enhanced leisure activities, perhaps we feel that there is no time to lose in reaching out to attain these objectives that lie, surely, just within our grasp. In this view, impatience is a virtue. We are simply filled with a zest for living life to the full as never before. A more open society allows both men and women a greater range of options in career, personal relationships and general lifestyle. The speed of technological advance gives us the feeling that nothing is ultimately beyond our eventual attainment. In this sense, the cry 'go for it!' captures so well our expectant and impatient attitudes.

On the other hand, in a less sanguine but perhaps more realistic frame of mind, we may come to see our contemporary impatience as being actually neurotic. It is hard to avoid altogether the feeling that we all rush about, trying to achieve the maximum in a minimum amount of time, because we are frightened that otherwise we will never get what we want. The nuclear disarmament lobby has been reminding us for years of our capacity for world annihilation. Relatively more recently, environmental concerns have been brought into public awareness. Specific details of the military scene and of the state of the environment may elude most of us, but the constant airing of these concerns acts so as to produce a certain public mood. This mood is the acknowledgement that our planet is very much a finite organism on which we are having a detrimental effect – we are fouling our nests, and there is the deep anxiety that the damage may be irrevocable.

Along with this exists the fear of our own mortality. How dreaded is the word 'cancer' for example, facing us with that total despair of utter non-existence and non-consciousness that death just might be. Right at the beginning of our exploration it was claimed that however a-religious our society seems to have become, nevertheless a personal sense of God's presence remains possible, and important, for many people. This being so we might expect to discover an equally general confidence in a continued existence after death. And in a way there is. As a parish priest I find when taking funerals that the majority of bereaved families evince a belief in the continuation of life. But what I also intuit is the thinness of this belief. They *need* to believe that the deceased person has not simply been snuffed out for ever and they *do* believe it. But the belief is somehow anaemic and debilitated. It represents thin ice and they are unwilling to risk their full weight upon it. Here a connection may be made with the experiences of Mrs T reported in Chapter 1. Her sense of God's presence in the silent church while arranging flowers mattered to her. But she refrained from pursuing its meaning: 'maybe I'm a coward, afraid of getting involved', she confided, 'I don't know'. Perhaps it is simply that we find it hard to justify our religious beliefs. Those beliefs remain of great personal importance to us, but we are careful not to expose them to open scrutiny. We hold them close to ourselves, aware that these thin tatters scarcely cover our nakedness, but holding them all the more tightly for their being our only clothing. Likewise, the popular belief in life after death is often a lone flag against a wide sky of fear of non-existence.

Might it be then the sense of the finiteness of our world and the anxiety about our own mortality that helps to account for our continual striving, restlessness and endemic impatience? If this interpretation is correct, then it will be as if the foundations of human life have been insidiously undermined: we pay lip-service to basic certainties, but we no longer feel that we can depend absolutely on them. This indeed is how it often feels. Both the dominance of empirical criteria for judging scientifically what is true, and the relativizing of religious beliefs, feed that human *despair* which Munch expressed in his paintings. We are alone. We have no absolute confidence in anything. So we must make the most of what we can do. 'Eat, drink and be merry for tomorrow we die'. Our impatience is neurotic in that it is a consequence of deep anxiety, but what we have lost cannot in fact be made up with hyperactivity. But we refuse to wait because we fear that there is nothing to wait for that we cannot have now, and we try to compensate for the loss of a future with a feverish acquisitiveness.

Our neurotic impatience is, to an extent, reflected in Christian worship and in our understanding of prayer. Most current forms of worship in this country, be they Anglican, Free Church or Catholic, are brief and busy. The charismatic movement, which has done so much to renew worship right across the denominational spectrum, has so far not instilled that attitude of patient receptiveness. Rather, it encourages us to get something from our worship *every* time, and thus we sing lots of choruses and shake hands enthusiastically to make sure that we do. Our snappy worship hardly encourages congregations to feel that the Sunday Eucharist is a time to wait on God. Instead, we are now the consumers, and it is so often the case that the loyalty of worshippers, sadly, tends to last only for so long as they continue to receive the goods.

The manner in which people participate in the Orthodox liturgy stands in marked contrast to our behaviour. The simple fact that it lasts for a good three hours may well puzzle British church members if, on a Greek holiday, they visit the local church on a Sunday morning. The art, the ritual and the music certainly provide a fabric for an uplifting of the heart and mind to the mystery of God. But the worshipper has to stand, and he has to subsume his own state of mind to a very corporate and official service *of* God. The objective validity of the liturgy itself hardly seems to require any subjective validation from individual worshippers. The worshipper places herself in the church and is thereby available to be woven into the fabric of the worship. She may not find the service inspirational, but she will know that she has been part of the Church's divine inspiration. As the stately action of the liturgy unfolds, people will come and go. The worshipper will enter, light a candle, kiss an icon or two, and then simply stand. There is in this attitude of worship a very noticeable absence of impatience. A sense of the utter reality of God seems to induce an openess to him, a willingness just *to be there*.

The private prayers of many Christians have undoubtedly been influenced by the resurgence of interest in the great contemplative tradition of the Christian Church. But this is not the only tradition to have been rediscovered. The healing ministry, with its roots in the actual practice of Jesus himself as shown in the Gospels, is also assuming primary significance for most mainstream Churches. Here, too, there are signs of a neurotic lack of patience. Without presuming to judge the validity of this ministry, we may notice the emphasis that is therein implicitly laid upon *results*. The more cautious and conservative-minded may discourage a rigid definition of what sort of 'healing' constitutes a result, but the implication of praying for a particular sick person is that it will effect some tangible improvement. It is all very well to explain that the laying on of hands is simply a symbolic expression of solidarity with the afflicted person, but the action itself is too easily identifiable with the intention that the GP will have on his visit: to repair and restore. For spiritual healing should be seen as just that: a fresh growth of the whole person in relationship with God. It can never be a merely ameliorative treatment of a particular physical or psychological ailment. Spiritual healing is secret, hidden and gradual – often not at all quantifiable.

The renewal of the healing ministry includes within itself a dangerous temptation, for it can be misused as a means for the contemporary Church to persuade those who view the Christian faith as an irrelevance that it can after all confer a direct and immediate benefit. We have intuitively learnt something from the advertising industry – that we will only sell our product if we direct our appeal clearly and seductively to the self-perceived 'needs' of the customer. Health is an ideally susceptible personal concern. Of course, this lesson has not been learnt in a cynically cold-blooded manner, but is it not true that Christians have unconsciously allowed the current concern for clearly discernible and fairly instant results to shape their gospel? This, obviously, is not meant as a wholesale condemnation of the healing ministry, for in its vision of the marriage between heaven and earth, body and spirit, it undoubtedly redirects us to the heart of our faith. What we *should* be very wary of is undue emphasis on the specific productiveness of the ministry.

An excessive expectation of immediate results is similarly displayed in the way in which some newer churches practise intercession. For example, in Donald English's book, *Ten Praying Churches*,[1] we hear from the Open Door Community Church in Uxbridge. Their pastor describes the success of an early-morning prayer meeting:

We have been amazed and delighted at the number of answers and obvious relevance of a prayer as we have read or heard the news. We pray about any major world event: that disasters may be reversed, corrupt dictators overthrown: for example, both Haiti and the Philippines have been rid of corrupt dictators recently, and we feel both were answers to prayer. . . . Five or six people have got just the kind of jobs they were seeking as we prayed, sometimes over a period of several months. With a number of single young people in the fellowship we often pray for flats and rooms to become available and find God faithful in answering our prayers.

Interestingly, the emphasis on results coincides for the Open Door Community Church with an apparent lack of appreciation of silence in their prayer. Earlier the pastor asserts, 'Everyone who prays needs to be physically and vocally active. Sitting in silence is the death knell of early morning prayer. We lift our hands . . . shout . . . clap . . . dance and leap . . . laugh . . . bow or kneel.'

Donald English is right when he urges us to learn from forms of prayer that may be radically different to our own. And one of the strong points of this particular approach is that it seems to be confirmed by the teaching of Jesus in the Gospels. Did he not say, 'If you ask anything in my name, I will do it' (John 14.14)? Many sermons, however, have dwelt on the meaning of 'in my name', suggesting that it represents not a magic key to automatic success in petition, but rather a precondition for meaningful prayer – that is, to become sympathetic with the mind of Christ. It cannot be wrong to teach that prayer, in the end, will be answered. But we need to be encouraged to take the long view of intercession. Between our asking and God's responding may lie a long period in which we grow in order to be able to receive God's response. Jesus taught, 'Ask, and it will be given you; seek, and you will find; knock, and it will be opened to you' (Matt. 7.7). Those words may too easily be read as an assurance of the effectiveness of prayer without noticing the due emphasis on 'ask', 'seek' and 'knock'. Asking, seeking and knocking require the hope of eventual success, but also forbearance and a trust in the God who, after all, knows best our human needs. Jesus himself, in the garden of Gethsemane, desperately asks – but is prepared to set his petition in the context of God's highest will. The crucifixion is the most dramatic example of the pain and the cost of such patience. We *are* boldly to ask, and insistently to knock on the door of the sleepy householder with whom Jesus humorously likened God. But we need to read between the lines of what Jesus is recorded to have said about petition, and realize that a certain hopeful resignation is as essential as the act of asking.

Intercession should be a priority in our private prayers, but the petition must always be allowed to float away on a sea of silence so that our personal concern is free to be woven into that outcome which is of the highest good. The laying on of hands will often seem to effect a wonderful healing, but an aspect of that wonder will be our inability to point to 'success' or 'results' in the realization that it is God's work. It would hardly be acceptable for the majority of British churches to adopt the Orthodox liturgy of St John Chrysostom for their regular Sunday worship – though it would be an interesting experiment! But the inclusion of silence in our own familiar forms of worship would help to induce the same sense of the priority and the givenness of the Divine mystery, and so encourage a corporate waiting upon God. In these ways, our cultural neurosis of impatience would be exposed as such and its subversive influence on our spirituality checked.

Michael Hollings relates, in a brief autobiographical sketch of his development as a Catholic priest, how he wrestled as a seminarian with the need simply to be available to God.[2] His account, personal and ruthlessly candid, shows how hard it is really to be patient and to wait on God:

> I set myself a routine of observing the *magnum silentium*, the silence following night prayers, when we were supposed to go to our rooms and not to talk to each other. There was a lot of temptation to go to coffee parties; not going, I came to feel isolated. I made a bedtime for myself, introduced sleeping on the floor and getting up to pray in the middle of the night. I rose early before the bell to get additional time for prayer. I also took to slipping away in the afternoon when many had a siesta or went walking. I located two churches which had exposition, one of which, S. Claudio in Piazza S. Silvestro near the English church, kept open all during the afternoon. There I often literally sweated it out, in dull, dumb, boring knee-aching slog. I slept there often; I seldom had much sense of prayer. Yet I went back there again and again, day by day, like a drowning man grabbing at a lifeline.

This, in hard realistic terms, is what we must expect the silence of waiting on God to be like if we wish to be weaned away from our impatience – 'dull, dumb, boring, knee-aching slog'.

We have to cultivate a prayer that goes against the grain of modern sensibilities with the acceptance that it may be quite unproductive, at least in the short term. In our struggle to maintain this (as it will feel) horribly passive state, the prayer of availability to God, it might help to borrow a strong visual image from the Buddhist religion.

This is the image of the Buddha seated cross-legged, hands, feet and facial expression held in contemplative poise. The image harks back to that moment when Gautama Buddha is said finally to have received enlightenment, sitting in meditation under a bo tree. It will help us, not in finding the path to Nirvana, for this is alien to our Christian faith, but in the attainment of a radical openness to God. Our detachment will be not a Buddhist detachment from the world of suffering and desire, but a very Christian detachment from self-centred restlessness as we learn confidently and trustingly to wait upon God. Even though it comes from a very different religious and cultural tradition, the Buddha image can speak strongly to Christians of the fundamental requirement simply to *be* before God. The serenity and tranquillity of this image will encourage us when the way is one of blood. sweat and tears, as it was for Michael Hollings.

It seems almost facile, though it is perhaps not so in our day, to say that waiting is a natural and inevitable human experience. The prenant woman waits a full nine months for the birth of her child. The farmer sows the seed and waits for harvest, trying not to curse the rain if there is too much or too little of it. The commuter waits on the station platform. His children wait for Daddy to come home at the end of the day. So much of our lives are spent between a promise and its fulfilment. This is exactly the biblical view of mankind's relationship to God. It gives us a vision of things to come – dramatically and symbolically in the Book of Revelation, more simply in the words of Jesus when he speaks of the coming Kingdom of God in terms of the potential of a tiny mustard seed. But these things that are surely to come remain at present merely a hope – and yet the seed has been planted. The New Testament views mankind as God's sowing which is already in the process of germination and growth. So the things that are to come are both 'not yet' and also, in their beginnings, 'now'. Thus Jesus speaks of the Kingdom of God as coming on a future day when 'you will see the Son of man seated at the right side of power, and coming with the clouds of heaven' (Mark 14.62). But this Kingdom is not far off. St Mark's Gospel opens with Jesus announcing that 'the kingdom of God is at hand', so we are to 'repent, and believe in the gospel' (Mark 1.15). St Paul sees this period between God's promise and its fulfilment as an almost cosmic process. 'We know that the whole creation has been groaning in travail together until now; and not only the creation, but we ourselves, who have the first fruits of the Spirit, groan inwardly as we wait for adoption as sons, the redemption of our bodies' (Rom. 8.22–23).

Here St Paul enunciates the key word 'wait', and he goes on to mention 'patience', explaining why these are indeed central qualities of Christian experience. 'For in this hope we were saved. Now hope that is seen is not hope. For who hopes for what he sees? But if we hope for what we do not see, we wait for it with patience' (Rom. 8.24–25). The natural silence of inevitable human waiting can be baptized into a thoroughly Christian prayer. We wait with hope and patience for that which we do not yet fully see. We still our anxious, neurotic impatience and let ourselves become dependent on God, waiting contemplatively on him. The Buddha image reminds us of the deep peace that can be enjoyed even in this waiting. A more biblical image is that from the end of the Book of Deuteronomy, when Moses is standing with God on top of Mount Pisgah. The journey is almost complete and the rich, fertile plain of the Promised Land is spread out below him. But God tells Moses that he will not himself enter this land, though the people will receive their inheritance as promised. This is a poignant moment, recapitulating the pain of the journey and anticipating the joy of the arrival. It is precisely this moment in extension that we Christians live, between the Divine promise and its fulfilment.

Moreover, the sort of waiting that Christians have quietly to accept is not merely that due to our particular place in the chronological scheme of things. The sense of living in a period between God's promise and its fulfilment is actually an inherent quality of personal encounter with God. There is something about our experience of him which is both 'now' and 'not yet'. When we meet God in silence we are interpreting the 'still dews of quietness' as hints of his reality. This sacramental approach, as we have learnt, allows a certain ordinary element to become a disclosure of the extraordinary. But we are not usually granted a full vision of God. In this sense, moments of silence remain oblique – albeit very powerful – indications of his reality. Thus we are forced to exist on a diet of intimations of God; we yearn to know him more fully, but he keeps us guessing. This, at least, is how it is for those of us who must deny that the Bible and Church tradition contain all the answers in a complete, instantly digestible form. The necessary application of reason opens our eyes to the interpretative function of this material.

The act of human judgement that it calls forth is always made on the basis of evidence that is somehow terribly compelling but also frankly ambiguous.

This makes life very hard for those who have an evangelistic ministry. If God presented himself a little more clearly to us, then it would be much easier to convince others of his existence and nature. Some try to evangelize as if the evidence were clear-cut. But those who accept this message in all good faith are then bound eventually to taste disappointment – and this may be a tragically destructive experience, foreclosing the possibility of future spiritual development for a long while. No, we must evangelize in a manner that is sympathetic to the content of our communication. If what we have, honestly, are intimations and hints of God, compelling but still ambiguous, then the mature evangelist will be less like a technician, diagrammatically explaining the structure of a particular construct, and more like a teacher encouraging his students to develop their own feelings about art and poetry. People have to enter into the spirit of the gospel until they can see these hints and intimations for themselves and feel the compulsion.

John Tinsley, Bishop of Bristol, wrote a stimulating and memorable article in 1980 entitled 'Tell it Slant',[3] in which he argued that the Christian faith is most faithfully communicated in a provocatively indirect style. The title comes from a poem by Emily Dickinson. 'Tell all the truth but tell it slant/ Success in circuit lies.' Bishop Tinsley suggested that our news about God has an irreducibly oblique quality. '*Telling it slant* is more than an appropriate form of the gospel; it is its essential content, a manner incumbent upon the Christian communicator by the very nature of the gospel. The gospel is not only *what* is said, but *how* it is said.' This is so, he explains, because we have not yet received a full revelation of God. What we know of God may be true, but it is also partial. The first few pieces of a jigsaw may give us sufficient clues as to be able to guess at the full picture. But we should be wary of jumping to conclusions and of assuming too much too quickly. 'All this is a reminder that revelation is provisional. The God who reveals is greater than what is revealed. God is not exhausted even in the Incarnation. This incompleteness, hiddenness, is indicated by signs, ambiguities, parables, ironies.'

Bishop Tinsley urges us not to gloss over these ambiguities in an effort to make the gospel more immediately understandable. This would only be to blunt the hints and clues and destroy their effectiveness. We have to strike a balance between the need to make sense, and the potential of the gospel material to hint at that greater whole that lies beyond our partial knowledge:

> When therefore Christians are dubbed 'hypocrites' there may be more truth in it than their critics realise. They are in one important sense dissemblers, seemingly devious in their indirection. The problem facing the Christian is how to be satisfactorily lucid, and yet leave enough implication for the gospel to reverberate in and through what is said.

Jesus himself taught in this way. We can imagine the silence that must often have followed his telling of a parable as his hearers allowed the story to reverberate. Although the closer disciples may later have been taken to one side for an explanation, Jesus is characteristically reluctant to spell out his meaning. 'To you it has been given to know the mysteries of the kingdom of God; but for others they are in parables, so that seeing they may not see, and hearing they may not understand' (Mark 4.11–12).

Parables, of course, by definition leave those being taught to draw their own conclusions. But so much of the teaching attributed to Jesus in the Gospels, when we examine it, is fresh and engaging by being pithy, imaginative – and inconclusive. For example, Jesus frequently refers to God as Father. But we are never provided with a complete, rounded picture of our Father in heaven. Instead, Jesus seems to let slip certain characteristics of the Father as he and his disciples go on their way. Thus if we look at just one of the Gospels, that according to St Matthew, we hear the Father being referred to in a multitude of epigrammatic ways. Each time a particular adjective or verb is applied, but the theme is never developed. The Father 'is perfect', rewards us, sees us 'in secret', is 'in heaven', will forgive us, feeds the common birds of the air, knows all that we need, has his own will, is 'Lord of heaven and earth', has a kingdom, inspires human behaviour, is glorious, has a face – which is always beheld by the angels in heaven – is our '*one* Father', and he knows all things. We end up with an intriguingly incomplete mosaic of the Father, but notice how this serves to present us with an invitation to know the Father better. The elliptical quality of Jesus' teaching awakens in us an appetite for further discovery. We are drawn into personal discipleship for a further unfolding of this essentially progressive revelation of the Father. 'All things have been delivered to me by my Father; and no one knows the Son except the Father, and no one knows the Father except the Son and any one to whom the Son chooses to reveal him' (Matt. 11.27).

Taking their cue from Jesus, present-day evangelists should be careful not to fall into the trap of thinking that they need to provide wall-to-wall information. This inevitably has a reductionist effect as available human ideas are substituted for the God who is reflected in, but who exceeds, present categories. It is much more in keeping with the actual nature of our knowledge of God to transmit provocative hints and compelling clues than to present volumes of systematic theology. The former are of course risky, while the latter are more secure in their illusion of completeness. But essential in the search for God is the willingness to step out into the less than immediately obvious.

However, it is all very well to say that this follows from our being set between the Divine promise and its fulfilment, the 'now' and the 'not yet', hints of God and the fullness of knowledge, and that we should try to cultivate a sense of patiently waiting on God in silence – but in this pious silence will inevitably grow the chagrined question 'Why?' Why does God seem to tease us so? Why does he keep himself tantalizingly hidden from full view? One may sometimes be able to persuade a small child to wait simply on the strength of one's own authority. But why precisely should we have to wait on God in this way? It should not be disguised that this is a fundamental and searching question to ask of Christianity, since it claims to be based on a self-revelation of God. The unavailability of a perfectly satisfying answer marks the problem itself, and constitutes the Christian's leap of faith. Our faith is that in the supreme wisdom of God there is some good reason for it, which we comfort ourselves with thinking will become apparent to us one day. But perhaps already the beginnings of an answer can be fashioned by analogy with the human nuturing of children. The wise parent recognizes the moment when she should refrain from directing the child exactly what to do. Of course, children have to be taught plainly and explicitly how to hold a knife and fork, how to cross the road, when to say please and thank you, and how to read. But then personal growth will be stunted if the child is denied the freedom to enjoy eating a meal without having Mum fussing over her, to cycle in the countryside with her friends, to go on her own to birthday parties, and to read widely the books of her choice. These activities are, in different ways, inherently risky. But children need the space to learn to do these things for themselves. The price of continued parental dependence is permanent immaturity. This represents the classic parental dilemma: How far should I direct, and when should I leave them to learn from their own mistakes? This is perhaps a dilemma shared by God. The space he grants to us may be frightening and indeed risky – but possibly essential if we are ever to attain spiritual maturity.

The analogy may be continued into the adult realm of ethics. God is hidden to us and elusive, just as certainty in human decision-making is often shot through with ambiguity. A believer may confidently proclaim his faith in God but, when challenged to explain in more detail what he means, find himself in an area of testing and experiment where each person has to make his own moves and live with the consequences. We become more and more aware that in human behaviour there are huge grey areas in which the conscientious often become caught in an agony of decision-making. Here we search in vain for neat, pre-packaged answers, for the onus is left on us to say what is right. Basic moral principles seem clear, but in their application clarity is often lost. For example, it is now technologically possible for a woman who has failed to conceive to be artificially fertilized, *in vitro*, by donor sperm. Could it be right for a barren woman, who is a committed Christian, to resort to this solution? Would she be breaking her marriage vows? Would the child be, in the way that God intends, the fruit of her marriage? Should it even be seen as an act of arrogant defiance against God who has, in his wisdom, ordained that this woman should not bear children? The Bible does not tell us what to do about *in vitro* fertilization, and it takes the Church a long while to make up its mind. But could it be that God deliberately refrains from telling us what to do in the knowledge that it is only our agonized struggle with such complex moral issues that will bring us to a greater maturity?

It is of course not particularly pleasant to be caught on the horns of such a dilemma, though most of us, to a greater or a lesser extent, do experience this at some time. Nor is it easy for those who feel that they are the guardians of a society's morals to accept that what is 'right' can only be established by way of numerous individuals making difficult personal decisions. The temptation is to denounce the 'relativism' of a degenerate liberal tendency, and forcefully appeal to God's already revealed instructions on the matter. But if it is true that God leaves us to decide for ourselves, then such an imposition will both be dishonest and will effectively prevent us from discovering what the more subtle rightness actually is in a particular case. The large grey area in human morality represents a space in which we are able to grow. Inevitably some horribly wrong decisions about, for example, *in vitro* fertilization will be made. But our willingness to allow the making of these decisions has the potential to promote our growth into a more moral society, with a greater sensitivity to the nuances of right and wrong. This is analogous to our understanding of the reality of God.

We experience only hints and incomplete intimations of God, and it is precisely this that sets mankind on the religious quest, the pilgrimage of faith. Though we can know but a little of God, when we do begin to taste him it is utterly compelling, and we then desire to reach out for him. An appetite to know God develops within us, to know even as we are known. The hiddenness of God creates a space. In this space our basic religious instinct first stirs and begins to push upwards into the light like a seed buried in the dark earth. But the manifestation of this light does not appear in its blinding fullness. Instead, the light is refracted and reflected from a multiplicity of angles. So gentle is the glow that at times it seems there is more of darkness than of light in the gloom. We marvel at its beauty, but we also question whether it has any enduring value or meaning. The freedom we have to do this, combined with the constancy of the light, allows our religious instinct to grow strong and mature. Too much light would burn it up, too little would cause it to be weak and sickly. Just the right strength, modulated by the One who waits for us to grow up to know him, both encourages us to lift up our hearts towards him and feeds us with sufficient spiritual nourishment.

Silent prayer acknowledges that emptiness which is our infuriating experience of God's apparent coyness in revealing himself to us. We simply *have* to learn to wait, even if at times we tap our fingers on the prayer desk in impatience. There is no hurrying this growth – any more than the farmer can speed up the growth of his corn by standing out in the field shouting angrily and waving his stick over the shoots. The growth will certainly occur, but imperceptibly and at its own natural pace. And that it does so is, in hindsight, a source of total wonder to us. 'And he said, "The Kingdom of God is as if a man should scatter seed upon the ground, and should sleep and rise night and day, and the seed should sprout and grow, he knows not how"' (Mark 4.26–27).

May we not affirm that in our contemporary society there is, on the part of those who hold aloof from organized religion, an honest recognition of the slowness of God to be revealed? Is it not felt that the Christian Churches have wanted to claim too much about God too quickly? In our defensiveness, do we not attempt to forcefeed new converts, when instead we should be being careful not to allow them to deny that space in which alone real growth can occur – and to which they will later inevitably revert by denying the Church? I think we must agree that, to some extent, this is so.

But what sort of God does this leave us free to present to the world? We may want to talk about the closeness and intimate care of a loving Father – to counteract a sense of God's remoteness and disinterest in our affairs, which talk about 'silence' and 'space' seems to encourage. There *is* perhaps a danger that the latter will lead to a new deism. Deism properly refers to that particular appreciation of God that grew out of the eighteenth-century Enlightenment, with its emphasis on the power of human reason. It was felt that reason alone could establish that God is truly 'the Intelligent Author of Nature' and 'the Moral Governor of the World'. There was thus no longer any need to pursue claims of Divine revelation. But neither was it felt that God intervened to disrupt the natural laws. So William Paley became famous for his suggestion that the mechanical regularity of the universe – like a watch that keeps perfect time – implies the existence of a Divine Watchmaker, which itself implies the independence of the watch, once wound, from its maker. God is the Superior Being whose existence is logically construed by intelligence, but who is now distanced from our world. Our latter-day deism may rest on the conviction that while we can indeed apprehend God, yet in its incompleteness this apprehension shows God to be remote from our immediate experience.

If our national religious attitudes are examined, it may well be felt that we have a certain natural tendency to deism in our make-up. The British reserve, that undemonstrative and cool but essentially polite way in which we treat each other, extends also to God. Enthusiasm only becomes more acceptable as public worship becomes a minority concern. Perhaps much that sociologists dignify as modern secularism can more easily be explained as our national religious temperament. It could be argued that our island experience of repeated invasion and assimilation bred an early indifference to the varieties of religion. But, whatever the historical antecedents of contemporary deistic attitudes, with roots trailing back into the eighteenth century and far beyond, it has to be acknowledged that the remoteness of God is also characteristically an ingredient of many honest people's religious experience today. This is not to contradict my initial and fundamental claim to the universality of a sense of the presence of God. It is to admit, though, that the sense of God's presence is mixed with, leads in and out of, what feels rather like the demureness of God. It would be unreal for Christians to deny this common experience. What we should do, however, is challenge the assumption that deistic reserve is a permanent feature. We must provide the positive interpretation of that distance from God as the space in which he allows us to grow. The apparent remoteness of God is a purely provisional quality directly analogous to the human parent who temporarily withdraws from her child so that he can learn, as he must, from his own experience.

So the deist assumes, perhaps sadly, or perhaps rather arrogantly, that God leaves us free to make our own decisions and to get on with our lives as best we can. The Intelligent Author and Moral Governor has set the world on its course and left it to its self-sufficiency. The Christian with a contemplative appreciation also accepts this area in which God remains unassertive. For him, God is not distant, but can be met in the depths of one's heart; the Divine presence is all-pervading, glinting now here, now there, as we detect him in all sorts of surprising places. But God does not impose himself: beyond the intimation of basic principles, he often seems not to tell us what to do; in the Scriptures, through the person of Jesus, by way of Church tradition and with the application of human reason, he provides us with but a fragmentary vision of himself. God has promised, and for those who trust his promise this is a time of waiting in which we see through a glass darkly. So our contemplative prayer will remind us both that we are expected to stand on our own two feet, and that all the resulting human activity is to be seen in the context of this waiting on God. The ultimate value of what we decide, of what we do, and even of what we seem to experience of him, waits for God's own evaluation. He is our Alpha and our Omega: between these two terms we listen and act and wait. To accept the natural silences of times when we feel thwarted, without impatience, *is* hard. It goes against the grain and conflicts with a God-given expectation of fulfilment. The cancer patient cries 'Why?' and is agonized at the apparent denial of her personal potential. Sometimes we are made to wait almost longer and more intensely than we can bear. But this has to be seen, in St Paul's words, as our 'groaning in travail . . . as we wait for adoption as sons'. To be silent in prayer *is* often painful; like Father Hollings, we sometimes have to wrestle with ourselves just to keep hold of the Divine promise.

Obviously, there are major intellectual obstacles to establishing a credible faith in a God who refrains from making himself immediately susceptible to human detection. God inevitably comes to be seen as an unnecessarily elaborate and, in the parlance of modern physics, inelegant hypothesis. But there is often also a major emotional obstacle. A child who is insecure cannot cope with too much independence from his parents. Only one who knows that she is properly loved, feels affirmed, has a fully intact self-esteem, and implicitly trusts her parents, can be safely granted the greatest freedom to learn her own lessons. Having some personal space may be the best way to learn, but it does presuppose an emotional maturity. As a general rule, those who were insufficiently loved as children tend to find it harder to establish satisfactory adult relationships. Is it not equally obvious that the degree of our present emotional maturity directly determines the quality of our relationship with God? If I feel lonely and unloved, thinking myself to be an unattractive middle-aged spinster, it will not be surprising if I want a God who is assertive, easily knowable and consolingly lovable, thus compensating me for my human loss. A God who issues his invitation – but then makes us wait with the minimum of consolation for the eventual party – may be hard to accept. If I have childhood memories of a father who drank, hit my mother, and sexually interfered with me, I shall find it hard to trust a God who now often seems suspiciously distant. I shall distrust any moments when he does seem to be present, wondering if for him too I am just a plaything to be used, abused, and finally ignored. It is much better to reject the existence of a God like this.

Moreover, the world cannot be clearly divided into those who have achieved emotional maturity and those who, sadly, remain immature. However well adjusted we may feel we are – able to hold our own in the light-hearted banter of a drinks party, able to relate to others easily and confidently – we nevertheless all have blindspots of emotional immaturity. We all have moments when we feel unloved,

undervalued and our self-esteem burns low. At such times our
feelings for God will be marked by a childish anxiety and over-
dependence. We act just like the small child who sobs wildly in a
moment of panic when her mother has suddenly to leave her to go
and bring the washing indoors. God encourages us to be grown up.
He leaves us to make our own big decisions so that we develop a fine
and subtle moral appreciation. He provides us with but a fragmentary knowledge of himself, so that our capacity for realizing the
Divine profundity unfolds to the full. But, all too often, we find the
resulting silence far too frightening to bear. In a world that
sometimes seems a jungle of threatening forces where we are keenly
aware of our human mortality, we need a God who comforts and
reassures. So we need to be aware that our relationship with God will
always be coloured by our propensity to cling. Our insecurity
constantly tempts us to impose pretended moral certainties in the
face of acute ethical dilemmas. We may not admit it to ourselves, or
to those whom we teach, but a two-dimensional cardboard cut-out
God is of more day-to-day use than the actual elusive Divinity. To
accept the space that God allows us for growth, to wait on him in
trust and confidence, calls – perhaps surprisingly – for courage. We
shall not always be up to it. Time and again we shall regress. But
each time God will hope to set us firmly and gently back on our own
two feet, again to listen and to wait patiently on him in the quietness.
The path of spirituality in our day consists in *not* succumbing to the
contemporary neurosis of impatience.

Confirmation of this view may be found in an examination of those
popular movements, commonly called 'fundamentalist', which seem
often to hit the headlines. When Islam is mentioned, everyone
thinks of the assertive creed of Iran (and we remain largely ignorant
of the equally influential, but gentle and mystical Sufi tradition
within Islam). It is common knowledge that more people appear
interested in religion in the United States than they seem to be in our
own country. But we look askance at the antics of tele-evangelists
and the more prominent born-again Christians, wondering if this
strange cultural divide could ever be bridged. We cannot help but
worry at the resurgence of an extreme revolutionary Islam in the
East, and of a dynamic but deeply conservative Christianity in the
West. In the first place we should avoid lumping all aggressive
religion under the heading 'fundamentalist' before we understand
the historically determined circumstances and the content of their

beliefs which give them this image. But it may be that what is called fundamentalism often identifies that universal human insecurity that we have been discussing. People in Iran are no less aware than those in America of the spectres of economic, military, social and environmental disaster. An increasingly stronger drug is needed to keep the fear of human mortality and twentieth-century angst at bay. The panacea is found in an unfailingly assertive God who judges those who do not immediately yield to his authority. This is a God who makes himself known. A critical study of the Koran has not been developed by Muslims any more than Christian creationists wish to encourage that sort of approach to the Bible.

Fundamentalist religion may strike liberal Westerners as unreal, being themselves unable to view reality in such black-and-white terms. But it is not so difficult to understand how a rigid pattern of thought can offer a reassuring sense of security. Characteristic of adolescence is the rallying around certain certainties – radical or conservative depending on what there is to be reacted against. Choosing a particular ideology for ourselves becomes an effective means of proclaiming our emerging personal identity. Since we are at that stage still rather shaky on our feet and inwardly terribly unsure of ourselves, the more strongly flavoured our chosen ideology is the better. Strident protestations effectively cover our own vulnerability; a total dependence on fundamental principles cloaks our personal uncertainty. Nor is this experience confined purely to adolescence. For example, most Christians find that there are periods in their lives when they seem to need a rest from the onward journey of spiritual pilgrimage. Then they seek the devotional equivalent of a comfortable armchair – and will probably not take too kindly to having this respite disturbed! Such a period may reflect a coming to terms with the so-called mid-life crisis when one has rather painfully to accept that one has now made one's major achievements. It may instead be a response to other, relatively minor, crisis: a fluctuation in the steadiness of a marriage; a dangerous threat to one's position at work from a younger person; the wild behaviour of one's teenage children. But at such times we feel in our individual selves something of the corporate insecurity that gives rise to religious fundamentalism.

Fundamentalist religion, whether Islamic or Christian, is regressive in that it takes us back to a more primitive concept of God, to that stern and reassuringly authoritarian figure on whom we can safely depend but which feeds upon our areas of emotional immaturity. An imposed spirituality, even if we accept the imposition with a joyful relief, denies us the space for growth. Here there will be no quiet waiting on God as our capacity for knowing him gradually develops. Instead, there will be shrill definitions that must obediently be accepted. Prayer will be, not a patient attendance on God in which we slowly and painfully discern the right, but a celebration of the great lawgiver. Not silence, but a constant praise, must fill the air, and the louder the better lest anyone should have the temerity to cry out that the emperor has no clothes on.

Nevertheless, just waiting on God *is* often extremely hard. In an age of neurotic impatience we have to swim against the tide, and the current is strong. We sometimes feel we need to *know* so badly, and then the temptation to give up the silence is almost overwhelming. How to practise this silent prayer of waiting on God? The most basic requirement is simply to *be there* before God. We have to force our minds not to run away with themselves, and it will be both symbolic and actually helpful if we can begin by keeping our bodies still. The image of the seated Buddha was referred to earlier, and a pose like that can itself be a form of Christian prayer. Dom J.-M. Dechanet, a Benedictine monk, taught how the Indian system of Hatha-Yoga can be used in precisely this way. In his encouragingly named book, *Yoga in Ten Lessons*,[4] Dom Dechanet said of silence:

> Silence is not prayer; but prayer, especially contemplative prayer, needs silence: in a sense it *is* silence that comes down from above or, with the help of a calm disposition, from the depths of the human heart . . . if we can escape the currents that sweep us on and the ideas that force us to live in a particular environment; if we can isolate ourselves, live by ourselves for a moment, several moments, the profound reality that makes us what we are, as Christians, must surely make its presence felt and lift up its voice within us.

Dom Dechanet saw that this silence requires a bodily stillness, and shows us how to harness Christian contemplation to Hatha-Yoga techniques. We are to begin by learning correct 'abdominal breathing':

Adopt a relaxed position.
    Lie flat on your back on the ground; stretch out quite straight on your rug . . . palms preferably turned upwards.

Relax in body and mind. Look up. Let your eyes rest on some part of the sky or ceiling. At first don't think about anything. Listen in complete detachment to the sounds that reach your ears.

After a minute or two, say to yourself: 'I am going to breathe slowly, as deep as I can.'

Then expel the air from your lungs, gently drawing in your stomach . . .[5]

Would it help to look for your own Hatha-Yoga teacher and so patiently learn how to enter the prayer of silence with your whole person? The tenseness and anxiety that afflicts most of us must indeed first be countered on a physical level. This will then allow a mental and spiritual poise in which we are able purely and simply to *wait* silently on God.

Notes

1 D. English, *Ten Praying Churches*. Eastbourne, MARC, Monarch Publications, 1989, pp. 79–80.
2 M. Hollings, *Living Priesthood*. Great Wakering, Mayhew-McCrimmon, 1977, p. 21.
3 J. Tinsley, 'Tell it Slant', *Theology*, May 1980.
4 J.-M. Dechanet OSB, *Yoga in Ten Lessons*. London, Search Press, 1965, p. 93.
5 ibid., p. 20.

5 · *Emptiness*

We may think that we live in an exceptionally noisy world, but in part that is because we avoid quietness. We become impatient in the emptiness of waiting; we prefer slick ready-packaged beliefs to a slow and vulnerable assimilation of them; through unfamiliarity we have become dulled to that inherent magic and beauty of utter silence that points beyond itself. It is perhaps our minimal experience of the hush that is a periodic feature of the natural world which helps to account for modern secular bafflement at the idea of God. Those who notice the quietness at dusk as the birds return to their nests; who stop and listen when they suddenly enter a clearing on a woodland walk; and who know the expectancy of those last few moments before dawn; they will have a greater natural susceptibility to sensing the reality of God. They will be more aware of the potency of this wonderful natural sacrament than those who live with the unending roar of a motorway in a constantly chattering environment. Stillness, just like the aesthetic enjoyment of beauty and the delight of human love, points powerfully beyond itself to God.

We have already had to leaven this appreciation with the admission that silence, when it *is* spiritually entered into, may be painful. We are exposed to a radical questioning of comfortable assumptions, we may have to face fearful inner forces of chaos and angst. At times it may seem that only a definitely affirmative articulation will save our faith – though we should always beware of too quickly glossing over the inner reality. We come now to make another, apparently negative, admission about spiritual silence. We have already explored the idea that God presents himself to us somewhat obliquely, keeping himself hidden, so that we have to wait for the fullness of faith. But we must also admit that there are times when God seems entirely *absent*. In a moment of acute personal distress we cry for help to God – and seem to be faced with an unyielding wall of silence. This is hardly an unfamiliar experience. We can all probably think of individuals who have felt rejected or let down by God in some particular personal crisis and who then have, perhaps we may feel understandably, rejected God.

In my work as a hospital chaplain it has become a familiar situation for me to be sitting at the bedside of a terminally ill patient together with one or two close relatives. Often such patients are able to come to a natural acceptance of their conditon, but not always. There are times when eyes look sharply at me from a gaunt face, stricken and wracked by illness. Words may not be spoken, but the dark despair and resentment is not hidden from this priest of God who dares to confront one who feels Godforsaken. The patient's husband or wife may turn his or her head to me in a mute appeal, knowing that we conspire in presuming to be hopeful even as life drains quickly away. Such glances are almost worse than the anguished question 'Why?', which often comes after the moment of death. 'Why did he have to suffer so much?' There is at least some comfort to be had in the fact that one has now actually commenced the process of adjusting to a hard fact. Sometimes it is only the physical event of death that is able to bring relief to a situation in which both patient and close relatives are tortured by the sense of utter meaninglessness. The bitterly articulated 'Why?' is at least a sort of prayer. Much worse is a silence of traumatized incomprehension, in which the sufferer feels that it is futile to raise her eyes to God, when any sense of God has been totally obliterated by feelings of anger and despair.

When a priest first experiences this type of situation there is a strong desire to be comforting and supportive. One struggles for words to say and looks for quick refuge in any possible action – such as saying a prayer or laying one's hand in blessing on the patient. Indeed, such a response is often appropriate and greatly appreciated – so far as it goes. It is all too easy then simply to leave the room, feeling that one has adequately performed one's priestly duty. This may be to avoid an area of profound anxiety, which has just been suppressed for a few minutes for the priest's benefit. It is not easy for one whose life is full to enter the utter emptiness of those whose expectations have all been blown away. In the hospital room where a person lies dying, painfully unreconciled to the inevitability of it, there can be moments of awful silence. At first there will be the numb silence of shocked disbelief when the news is gently broken to the patient. Then there is the existential silence as non-being is contemplated. A spiritual silence ensues if the patient feels (and who would not?) that prayers have not, and are *still* not, being answered. Later in the day there will probably be an implicit silence as visiting friends and family skirt carefully around the truth. 'Oh, we'll soon have you out of here!' Over the broken glass of these silences steps the chaplain, only to add his own as he sits there wondering what on earth to say.

This is not a silence we care to explore. We are reminded of our own mortality. We feel professionally incompetent. We perceive the limits of our own faith. Our natural reaction is either not to take the silence seriously, or not to stay with it for very long. It is sometimes surprisingly hard simply to reach out, to take the patient's hand and remain there for a while. Often the most authentic comfort that can be given is to show that someone else has recognized the silence and is prepared to share it for a bit, to travel along with the sufferer. Patients who receive some bad news about their condition later describe the experience as feeling cut off from the normal world. People come and go, the ward routine continues, but they are cocooned in a private silence where all that makes for personal meaning is suspended. It is not a congenial experience for the priest to seek to empathize with this state in which the patient feels frighteningly insulated from normal social reality. But one some-times has to struggle to overcome one's natural resistance and try to achieve this in some measure. To do this I find I have to remind myself of my own humanity. I approach the patient not as a representative of God, with my book of wisdom and bag of sacramental aids, but as a fellow human being who could very easily find himself in the same boat. We can all know what it is to feel abandoned by God, and perhaps this is where a genuine priestly ministry must begin. Disturbing as this is, none the less I feel immensely privileged as a hospital chaplain: sharing such experiences enables me, in my comfortable well-being, to attune my ear to the silences of God.

Having a son suddenly killed in a motorcycle accident; being diagnosed as having cancer; losing one's life partner: such experiences will inevitably affect our relationship with God. We shall feel confronted with the impotence of God in allowing this thing to happen in the first place; and we will probably be filled with anger, loss and despair when it seems that God is going to do nothing to set things right again. Sometimes one's faith is totally undermined. Certainly God can never be seen in the same light again. Such times

of crisis act as prisms which refocus our image of God. A wholly new
dynamic is introduced into our relationship with God when a sense
of belonging to him is seen not to preclude the most intense
suffering. It is at this point that we need to re-examine the
crucifixion of Jesus, and especially his cry, 'My God, my God,
why? . . .' (Matt. 27.46). We have to admit the truth that being loved
by God does not stop nasty things happening to us. This may not
seem much of a revelation, but the cross is displayed everywhere as
the primary symbol of Christianity. We all, to some extent, have to
taste for ourselves the silence of that darkness which held sway over
the whole land from the sixth until the ninth hour. The absence of
our God will serve, one way or another, as a crucible of truth.

In modern history the Jewish holocaust of the Second World War
is the most acute example of people with faith in God being faced, in
their extremity, with the silence of God. The writings of Jews who
survived the concentration camps must now be allowed to shape our
contemporary Christian conception of God. Such writings tell the
most powerful parables of the tension between suffering and faith.
Elie Wiesel, for example, was born in Romania in 1928. When aged
fourteen, he became swept up in the deportation of the people of his
ghetto to the Nazi concentration camp at Auschwitz. In his book,
Night,[1] he presents a personal record of this childhood nightmare.
In its honesty, artlessness, immediacy and pure horror it is the most
disturbing book I have ever read. The reader is able to enter the
camp with Wiesel and survey the scene through the eyes of a
frightened Jewish lad clutching his father's sleeve. Wiesel tells how,
upon leaving the train, they were met by some resident prisoners. As
they filed slowly forward, one urged the boy to tell the soldiers that
he was eighteen, another exclaimed, 'Poor devils, you're going to the
crematory'. Then Wiesel saw the flames for himself and realized, for
the first time, the enormity of what was actually happening. This
moment of realization was to be the turning point for him, though,
not surprisingly, his mind initially rejected what his eyes seemed to
see:

Not far from us, flames were leaping up from a ditch, gigantic
flames. They were burning something. A lorry drew up at the pit
and delivered its load – little children. Babies! Yes, I saw it – saw
it with my own eyes . . . those children in the flames. (Is it surprising that I could not sleep after that? Sleep had fled from my eyes.)

So this was where we were going. A little farther on was another and larger ditch for adults.

I pinched my face. Was I still alive? Was I awake? I could not believe it. How could it be possible for them to burn people, children, and for the world to keep silent? No, none of this could be true. It was a nightmare.... Soon I should wake with a start, my heart pounding, and find myself back in the bedroom of my childhood, among my books ...

There was, of course, no waking from this nightmare. Wiesel felt that he would prefer to throw his body against the electrified perimeter fence then to die slowly in the flames. He turned to tell his father so, but his father could not answer:

He did not answer. He was weeping. His body was shaken convulsively. Around us everyone was weeping. Someone began to recite the Kaddish, the prayer for the dead. I do not know if it has ever happened before, in the long history of the Jews, that people have ever recited the prayer for the dead for themselves.

'Yitgadal veyitkadach shme raba.... May His Name be blessed and magnified ...' whispered my father.

It was at this point that Wiesel, young scion of God's ancient people, asked the question so pertinent to all future human experience of God and so definitive for our quest here. 'For the first time, I felt revolt rise up in me. Why should I bless His Name? The Eternal, Lord of the Universe, the All-Powerful and Terrible, was silent. What had I to thank him for?'

It is the fact that Wiesel was such a serious and devout young Jew, already drawn to mysticism, that gives this question such authority. He spoke for all who have ever, in their innocence and without any justification, suffered terribly. He articulated the cry of all those who have come trustingly to depend on God and yet find themselves alone in their hour of desperate need. It must have taken great moral courage for Wiesel to ask this question: to have had such awful honesty in confessing the terrible silence of God. In a sense, Wiesel, though he survived the death camps, was destroyed by this question and the situation from which it arose. His soul burnt up in the intensity. But his words still burn with fire, witnessing to a Divine silence the significance of which must never be forgotten. 'Never shall I forget that nocturnal silence which deprived me, for all eternity, of the desire to live. Never shall I forget those moments which murdered my God and my soul and turned my dreams to dust. Never shall I forget these things, even if I am condemned to live as long as God Himself. Never.'

From the early fathers to modern theologians, many attempts have been made to meet this supreme challenge.[2] Not one has succeeded in producing a wholly satisfactory rational explanation. Reason alone cannot, it would seem, rescue belief in God from the great question mark of suffering and evil. The sheer scale and utter wastefulness of the agony and loss suffered in Auschwitz and Buchenwald reminds us how impossible it is to suggest that this could somehow tie in with a greater purpose. Just what could redeem the terror and the screams of those women and children as they arrived by the trainload? Suffering like this does not ennoble the soul of man. And if it is judged to be a tragic possibility of human freedom, then must we not accept the implicit cruelty (or at least, amorality) of that freedom? Perhaps the most enduring religious response to the problem of suffering is that which refrains from offering a complete explanation of God's purposes – and yet stubbornly affirms that we must continue to trust in his goodness. This response derives from the fact that even when the reality of human suffering is taken wholly seriously, there is *sometimes* something in the believer that speaks of the love and presence of God. Outward events would seem to deny God, yet in the depths of the heart (if it is not, like Wiesel's, just too damaged) a joyful song of hope may still be heard.

Essentially, this is the message of the Book of Job in the Old Testament. The apparent cruelty of God's testing of Job, and the hard injustice of Job's undeserved suffering, remains unjustified and unresolved. The Lord, in fact, does not give Job a reasonable answer when he speaks to him out of the whirlwind. What *is* significant is that Job arrives at a moment when, despite all that has happened to him, he re-encounters God himself. 'I had heard of thee by the hearing of the ear, but now my eye sees thee' (Job 42.5). This experience does not explain or justify his suffering, but it does restore his relationship with God. This may seem strange, or merely weak, but it actually represents the final position of many theologians who have tried to justify the ways of God to man. Hans Küng, for example, reaches this ultimate conclusion:

Yes, to cling to him even in an absolutely desperate situation, simply empty and burnt out, when all prayer dies out and not a word can be spoken: *a fundamental trust of the most radical kind*, which does not externally appease anger and indignation but encompasses and embraces them, and which also puts up with God's permanent incomprehensibility.[3]

Even when we are indignant at God's inaction in the face of vast numbers of infant deaths through malnutrition; even when we cannot find a word to bring the suffering cancer patient to God; even when, with the death of one's child, we are disgusted with any form of prayer; yet there may be something in us that is able to *cling*. What this boils down to is that while on the one hand theologians have consistently failed to justify fully God's inaction, yet on the other hand, even when human suffering is taken seriously, God's love and presence remain to be encountered. Usually this last point is emphasized and an appeal made to that 'fundamental trust of the most radical kind'. Christians cannot answer the 'Why?', but in the name of the suffering Christ they can continue to trust in a loving God. But the former point (that we fail to justify God's inaction) needs *also* to be emphasized. The trouble is that we inherit a philosophical conception of God who is by definition all-powerful. The time has come for us to talk honestly about God's impotence. It is pig-headed to ignore the reality of human experience, daft to insist that God is really in control, when we know that in our moment of desperation God was painfully silent.

Perhaps we are afraid that to admit this will lead to an undermining of our faith, or that it is tantamount to a blasphemous rejection of 'Almighty God'. I do not believe that this is so. As for the latter, God is big enough to survive our human questioning; and as for the former, our relationship with him will only be deepened if we honestly and vulnerably open our hearts. What must be made totally clear at this point is that we should not assume that this pilgrimage of faith will reveal God as he is in himself, but only God as he chooses to relate to us. With this paramount qualification, we can now allow ourselves to learn freely from the Jewish descent into a Nazi hell, reflecting and recapitulating as this does the complete history of innocent human suffering in which God has seemed despairingly silent. We shall connect the apparent impotence of God with the Christian capacity to trust in his love and goodness none the less. In doing so, we shall simply be taking human experience seriously and seeking to relate it to what we have received in the religious tradition. This task requires a strong stomach in its twin commitment, for in this area it is rather more usual to keep a safe operating distance between experience and tradition.

Those who have had the moral courage to question the justice of God enable us all to penetrate the tissue of notions and feelings that represent God as we would have liked him to be. It may seem utterly arrogant on our part, or indeed dangerously liberating, to accuse God himself, but if we are driven by honesty and not hubris this questioning will lead to fresh discovery. We need to contemplate as fully as we can the silence of God in the face of human suffering. That it is virtually impossible for all but the most remarkable of individuals to sustain this interrogation for long, shows how quickly most of us succumb to an easy comfort and reassurance. Fyodor Dostoevsky was, however, one such individual. In his novel *The Brothers Karamazov*,[4] Ivan's conversation with his brother Alyosha, so often quoted in discussions of this theme, presents sharply the judgement that lurks hazily at the back of so many minds. Ivan judges that present suffering could not possibly be a fair price for future glory: 'If the sufferings of children go to make up the sum of sufferings which is necessary for the purchase of truth, then I say beforehand that the entire truth is not worth such a price.... We cannot afford to pay so much for admission. And therefore I hasten to return my ticket of admission.' Ivan assures Alyosha that he is not rejecting God, but merely the injustice of his creation. 'It is not God that I do not accept, Alyosha. I merely most respectfully return him the ticket.'

Despite this disclaimer, Ivan knows that he has made a most damaging censure of God. If creation is to be judged an immoral system, then it is clearly God who is blameworthy. Ivan goes on to describe to Alyosha a poem he has written, in which is expressed the horror and tragic irony of humankind condemning God. In this poem God spontaneously determines upon a second earthly incarnation. He appears quietly in Seville, but is instantly recognized by the people. 'The people are drawn to him by an irresistible force, they surround him, they throng about him, they follow him. He walks among them in silence with a gentle smile of infinite compassion.' On the very steps of Seville Cathedral, he encounters a child's coffin emerging after a funeral. Her mother recognizes him and appeals for

help. 'He gazes with compassion and his lips once again utter softly
the words, "Talitha cummi".' Suddenly the cardinal appears, the
Grand Inquisitor. He considers the scene. 'He sees everything. . . .
He knits his grey beetling brows and his eyes flash with an ominous
fire. He stretches forth his finger and commands the guards to seize
him.' Deep in the vaults, the Inquisitor goes to his Prisoner.

> Amid the profound darkness, the iron door of the prison is
> suddenly opened and the old Grand Inquisitor himself slowly enters
> the prison with a light in his hand. He is alone and the door closes
> at once behind him. He stops in the doorway and gazes for a long
> time, for more than a minute, into his face. At last he approaches
> him slowly, puts the lamp on the table and says to him:
> 'Is it you? You?'
> But, receiving no answer, he adds quickly: 'Do not answer, be
> silent. And indeed, what can you say?'

This extends our understanding of God's silence when the sufferer
ineffectually cries out to him. Is this silence that of God who chooses
for his own inscrutable yet good purposes not to rescue the petitioner;
or in fact a silence that betokens Divine guilt, indicating that to such
accusations God has no defence, can have nothing to say?

Dostoevsky succeeds in taking us to the heart of the matter. The
means are brutal and shocking, and once there he does not propose
any simplistic resolution of the pain. He encourages us to search
even more intently for the meaning of that silence to which Ivan's
apparently successful prosecution opens our ears. Ivan's Grand
Inquisitor speaks out after a silence of ninety years. As he listens to
the story, Alyosha wonderingly asks his brother, 'And is the
Prisoner also silent? Does he look at him without uttering a word?'
Now that we have been brought to this point, are we to say that
the silence is simply that of moral culpability? But we should note
the inexplicable character of this silence. Why does the Prisoner,
second incarnation of God, *not* speak in defence and illumination?
Could this muteness actually be a continuation of that previously
described, when he walked among the townspeople of Seville 'in
silence with a gentle smile of compassion'? And this brings us fully
to the heart of the problem that believers encounter in innocent
human suffering. Despite God's apparent impotence, it is not
possible to write him out of the story. Even in the most terrible

Godforsaken hurt, God is there to be met – even if it is as the Prisoner, seemingly so justly accused.

When a person suffers, and appeals to God from the depths but receives no help, he becomes the most vulnerable, pitiable victim. What is so acutely ironic, and in the moment of suffering perhaps profoundly unhelpful, is that a primary Christian image of God is that of the suffering Christ. The victim cries out to God for rescue, not realizing that God is to be found as a fellow victim. In the Book of Job, God apparently enters the story in chapter 38 when the Royal Voice issues from the clouds. Or is this a naïve conclusion, the product of an immature religious consciousness? Job may picture God as the cause of his suffering and his final vindication, but if this explanation is for us just too obviously contrived to be credible, we ought to look again at the three friends. At the very beginning of the account, in chapter 2, they make the most authentic response of the whole book to Job's pain. Seeing him from afar they weep, tear their robes, and sprinkle dust upon their heads. 'And they sat with him on the ground seven days and seven nights, and no one spoke a word to him, for they saw that his suffering was very great' (Job 2.13). We will be angry if God remains silent when we cry to him in real personal distress; we are indignant at his inaction as millions of children starve to death: but we have to see that this awful silence speaks also of a God who enters totally into his people's suffering. He may not help, but he is *there* with us. We can now begin to make sense of that 'fundamental trust of the most radical kind' of which Küng wrote, 'which does not externally appease anger and indignation but encompasses and embraces them'.

Returning again to Wiesel's personal account of Jewish suffering in the concentration camps, we should look carefully at one passage that evokes a peculiarly Christian response. In it the question is asked, 'Where is God now?', and whether or not Wiesel received it, perhaps an answer *is* given. The passage concerned reports the hanging of three prisoners, two adults and a child:

> The three victims mounted together on the chairs.
>   The three necks were placed at the same moment within the nooses.
>   'Long live liberty!' cried the two adults.
>   But the child was silent.
>   'Where is God? Where is He?' someone behind me asked.

At a sign from the head of the camp, the three chairs tipped over. Total silence throughout the camp. On the horizon, the sun was setting.

'Bare your heads!' yelled the head of the camp. His voice was raucous. We were weeping.

'Cover your heads!'

Then the march past began. The two adults were no longer alive. Their tongues hung swollen, blue-tinged. But the third rope was still moving; being so light, the child was still alive. . . .

For more than half an hour he stayed there, struggling between life and death, dying in slow agony under our eyes. And we had to look him full in the face. He was still alive when I passed in front of him. His tongue was still red, his eyes were not yet glazed.

Behind me, I heard the same man asking:

'Where is God now?'

And I heard a voice within me answer him:

'Where is He? Here He is – He is hanging here on the gallows . . .'

That night the soup tasted of corpses.

Wiesel implies that his faith in God was annihilated, rendered lifeless, in that moment just as, agonizingly, cruelly and irrevocably, life was quenched in that child. How *could* anyone believe after being forced to look into the very eyes of the child? Yet when a Christian reads this passage an association with Christ's crucifixion will inevitably be made. The three figures hanging in that concentration camp become a horrible *alter imago* of Calvary, which is perpetuated time and again throughout history. The emptiness that filled Wiesel's soul as he gazed at the scene reminds us of what Mary must surely have felt when she stood at the foot of the cross. The child's slow dying represents the three hours of darkness and the man's anguished question echoes Christ's cry, 'Eloi, Eloi, lama sabachtani?' But for Christians, the human suffering of Jesus signifies the total love of God for humanity. God enters thoroughly into the human condition, somehow taking into himself our darkest fears and our cruellest agonies. The crucifixion says: in the midst of pain, despair and terror there is God. To the Christian, Wiesel's answer is ambiguous: God indeed is here, hanging on the gallows. Faith in God may be not destroyed, but metamorphosed. In the concentration camp God remained silent, but was not absent. He was, however, not easily recognizable: the Omnipotent in the impotent suffering of a child.

Even Christians find it hard to see God in the Prisoner, or in the three friends of Job who (at first) can have nothing to say.

Earlier we reached an appreciation of the natural silences of our world as sacraments of God's presence, moments of contemplation becoming points of divine disclosure. Can we now see that even that silence which at first seems to signify God's failure can be invested with a sacral power? We can only do so if we can bear to allow the cosy world of piety to be turned upside down and ransacked. We aspire to a God who is transcendent, in our imaginations radiant with Divine beauty, the highest principle of Being. But if we are truly to cope with the depths of human experience we must be prepared to discover God relating to us as humiliated and contemptible, with 'no form or comeliness that we should look at him . . . as one from whom men hide their faces' (Isa. 53.2,3). If we cannot do this we shall ultimately find our silent contemplation of God turning bitter and finally drying up. The joy of encountering God's presence is not a sauce to make ordinary life more palatable; rather, it leads us into the depths of our human condition and there gives us hope.

I repeat again that we should not presume to think that our pilgrimage of faith reveals God as he is in himself, but only God as he chooses to relate to us. Nor has anything I have said thus far succeeded in justifying the ways of God to man. In the midst of intense human suffering God remains silent. Why? We cannot say. What we can say is that even this most agonizing of silences, by virtue of being powerfully ambiguous, can become sacramental to God's presence. Furthermore, *this* presence may cause us to revise our understanding of Divine presence as experienced heretofore. A barren emptiness replaces that stillness which had seemed full of the reality of God; but then, in the very disillusionment of our loss, the emptiness discloses One who has most intimately identified himself with us. This transposes us from a state that is perhaps little more than aesthetic enjoyment, into a genuine spirituality, for we are drawn into the heart of God's love for us and, in our utter vulnerability, invited to respond.

Yes, this understanding of God's involvement in human life is highly questionable. Is a God who appears to us so passive worthy of our respect? Is it not contradictory to associate any form of weakness with God? What sort of salvation does it leave us to hope for? But our emphasis here is experiential rather than merely theoretical. Honest attention to our actual worldly experience of God may finally provide some answers to those questions. In the meantime, we may be encouraged by those theologians who themselves refused to sacrifice their raw humanity to an intellectual vision of God. Dietrich Bonhoeffer wrote of God from his prison cell in Second World War Germany, having vigorously opposed discrimination against Jews and courageously participated in the struggle against Nazism. We should not be surprised if the deprivations of imprisonment, separation from supporters, family and fiancée, had led him to feel abandoned by God. Perhaps they did. But Bonhoeffer wrote of God as a fellow sufferer, who will be experienced as having forsaken us, but who is in reality being abased with us – and is *in this way* most powerfully and definitively *with* us:

> ... our coming of age leads us to a true recognition of our situation before God. God would have us know that we must live as men who manage our lives without him. The God who is with us is the God who forsakes us (Mark 15.34). The God who lets us live in the world without the working hypothesis of God is the God before whom we stand continually. Before God and with God we live without God. God lets himself be pushed out of the world on to the cross. He is weak and powerless in the world, and that is precisely the way, the only way, in which he is with us and helps us. Matt. 8.17 makes it quite clear that Christ helps us, not by virtue of his omnipotence, but by virtue of his weakness and suffering.[5]

Much earlier, the brilliant but controversial philosopher and theologian of the twelfth century, Peter Abelard, had developed a version of the atonement that proceeded in much the same direction.[6] He taught that the innocent suffering of Christ on the cross was the supreme example to lead mankind in the way of love, forgiveness and personal generosity. God gave totally of himself with but the hope that this would win a reciprocal response from his people. Abelard has been accused of reducing the particular significance of the crucifixion as *the* turning point in our relationship with God into a moment that simply revealed a general truth about God. But the value of his interpretation is that he did not attempt to pretend that the suffering and desolation of the crucified Christ were really just a means for the eternal and powerful God to accomplish his will for humankind. Instead, he took seriously the failure and emptiness of Calvary. One feels that Abelard must have begun his theology of the cross from his own personal experience of rejection and pain. It clearly mattered to him that God himself was to be found in our world of hopelessness and affliction. If such a failure as the torture and death of Christ was to have any meaning, it would be in the more deeply compassionate response that it might subsequently generate in the hearts of men. Abelard knew that whatever pain he had to endure, God in Christ could *there* be found.

The contemporary theologian Jurgen Moltmann[7] has developed this same theme in a manner that seems no less refereshing and meaningful – and perhaps also shocking – today. Like Abelard, he fully acknowledges the human dereliction of the cross, but goes on to stress that Christ's worst suffering was the sense of having been cast off by God. 'The suffering in the passion of Jesus is abandonment, rejection by God, his Father.' And what this actually means, Moltmann argues, is that God himself is fully incarnated into our human experience of feeling Godforsaken. 'When God becomes man in Jesus of Nazareth, he not only enters into the finitude of man, but in his death on the cross also enters into the situation of man's godforsakenness.' That God chooses to do this is an inevitable consequence of his love for us: 'a God who is incapable of suffering is a being who cannot be involved ... the one who cannot suffer cannot love either'. What makes Moltmann's theology of the cross so vivifying is its ability to engage with the most painfully negative parts of our human condition. Just *there* is where God is to be encountered. God encompasses our human hurts, is able truly to put his arms round us, because he has these same hurts in his own heart. Moltmann manages this with honesty and without any sense of contrivance. He acknowledges the experience of Godforsakenness in which, paradoxically, can be discovered the presence of God. He does not yield to the temptation of constructing some artifice which might superficially explain away the former in terms of the latter. He allows us to confess *both* our sense of Godforsakeness *and* also the Divine presence.

The key scriptural text for the articulation of this experience of God comes in the second chapter of the epistle to the Philippians:

> His state was divine
> yet he did not cling
> to his equality with God
> but emptied himself

> to assume the condition of a slave,
> and became as men are,
> and being as all men are,
> he was humbler yet,
> even to accepting death,
> death on a cross.

These words are set in the form of an early Christian hymn, so it is to be read as a serenade of the God who is encountered after baptism in Christ – and expressly not as a cool philosophical definition of God in his second Person. Nevertheless, it provides us, I suggest, with the definitive model for understanding the manner in which God chooses to relate to us in terms of our own experience. If we look for one who is Divine, we may miss the one who is as a slave. Out of the depths we cry to the great God to come and save us; this attitude does not predispose us to notice the presence of the one who, like ourselves, is totally emptied.

This idea of the self-emptying of the Divine nature has never been fully explored in Christian theology. Its usefulness in interpreting the Divine nature of Christ has at various times been experimented with, for example by Bishop Gore in the nineteenth century. But to such attempts some fairly obvious objections have always been quickly levelled. Would it not be impossible for God to cease being God? Or, if it is said that the Son laid aside some Divine attributes while the Father continued as ever, would it not be incoherent to think that God could be divided? However, the real value of the notion of God's self-emptying is not in its providing an ingenious, mechanistic explanation of the incarnation. Instead, we should learn to sing this ancient hymn for ourselves. Its lyrics, issuing from the spring of early apostolic experience, sing of one whose love for mankind and desire to be utterly available, entail a lowliness and humility quite unexpected by us. If the hymn now presents a theological problem that is because it catches, quite ingenuously, a profound truth witnessed by those who first followed the Lord. This was the extraordinary feeling that the Lover abandons himself to the beloved. We meet him as the servant who sits us down at table and waits mutely on us; in times of despair we are not to cast our eyes heavenwards, but need look no further than our fellow-sufferer.

The great danger in singing this hymn, while mankind groans under its burden of suffering and God remains silent, is that it might seem merely facile. The reassurance that God fully shares one's sufferings can sound awfully glib, especially when the comforter steps easily away from the situation. We must make quite sure that we do not underestimate the extreme costliness of Divine self-emptying: for God himself, for the sufferer, and indeed for the pastor who is really prepared to share the silence. The Frenchwoman Simone Weil, philosopher, teacher, idiosyncratic religious thinker, wrote of God's self-renunciation that was to be encountered at the heart of creation. In her own spiritual turmoils she felt that she had suffered that silence which is the result of God having given of himself. And this is not peaceful quietness, but instead an agonizing tearing apart of God:

> God created through love and for love.... He created beings capable of love from all possible distances. Because no other could do it, he himself went to the greatest possible distance, the infinite distance. This infinite distance between God and God, this supreme tearing apart, this agony beyond all others, is the crucifixion.... This tearing apart ... echoes perpetually across the universe in the midst of the silence, like two notes, separate, yet melting into one, like pure and heart-rendering harmony.... When we have learnt to hear the silence, this is what we grasp more distinctly through it.[8]

Weil was right. We have to speak of discovering God as one who is passive and vulnerable, but if this is a result of his passionless unconcern then it would be the negation of God. God is silent because in his supreme commitment to creation he is torn apart by the strength of his love. 'God so loved the world that he gave' (John 3.16). Weil wrote of a void that we must allow and make room for at the centre of human experience: this emptiness is the suffering of God. When *we* suffer and cry out for help, but find only silence, then it is in that that we touch God himself. Weil lived her life deliberately just beyond the pale of Christianity, continually agonizing over the desirability of baptism and always shrinking from cosy religious affirmations and pious comforts. Longing at times to enter the Church, she could not help but feel that this would be to concede to that which was less than God. Christians speak of a need to be Christ-centred, but Weil succeeded in keeping herself centred on the void. 'The world must be regarded as containing something of a void in order that it may have need of God.'[9] Weil's own bitterness and ambiguity reminds us that not for one moment should we suppose experience of the void to be anything less than a taste of God's own tearing apart: to acknowledge God's silence is to be torn apart ourselves.

The human cry 'Why?' echoes in the silence of God's inaction. I have tried to suggest that this, the very worst of silences, is itself pregnant with the message of God's love. It is perhaps only when we have truly known the absence of God that we can authentically encounter his presence, and become able to tell the difference from those religious emotions that we conjure up for ourselves. Not to sense the reality of God at a time of personal pain produces real anguish, but this most awful experience can, in an utterly mysterious manner, flower into a sacrament of the Divine reality. In saying this, are we perhaps exploiting and abusing the integrity of those such as Wiesel in their reported experiences? Are we answering their extreme righteous indignation with a platitudinous 'Never mind, God understands and shares your pain – it will all come right in the end'? By no means. It is precisely our inability to discern any greater purpose in innocent human suffering that forces us to face the absence of a benevolent Deity; but then, in listening some more, to pick up traces of a Suffering Servant. Wiesel relates his experiences, and his own personal conclusions, with total honesty and integrity, and for this he commands our deepest respect. But it is for us to reflect further and to do our theology in the light that he has cast. The image of that child hanging on the gallows, dying slowly into a silent sunset, may generate the sloughing off of much that we have previously meant by 'God'. We have to ingest, *but make our own*, Wiesel's raw 'Where is God? He is here'.

Or is this all just so much wishful thinking? Is it merely a rather elaborate cop-out created by reason of our not being able to cope with the meaninglessness of human suffering and the absence of a reassuring Providence? In the first place, we must have total honesty: like Wiesel, like Dostoevsky, and like the priest who sits often at the bedside of terminally ill patients. We must be true to the actual data of the human experience of suffering – our pain and God's silence. But we shall know that particular beliefs are always used to interpret such data. The Jew, the Christian, the agnostic, the atheist, each will have their particular expectations. These beliefs will, in turn, be judged by their adequacy in interpreting the data. If one has believed that there is no transcendental meaning or purpose because there is no God, then the silence in which one suffers will be utterly empty and lonely. If this is almost beyond endurance one will naturally listen to the cosmic silence as never before. Is it quite empty? If, as Christian or Jew, one has accepted an authoritarian, paternalistic image of God, then the non-response to one's most desperate prayer may provoke a crisis of faith. Some frightening question marks begin to manifest themselves. In this extremity, that part of the tradition that treats of God's sympathy and tenderness for his people will alone have credibility. One may be able to retain only a strange vision of the utterly crucified love of God. But this may be the key that finally turns the lock of human torment and opens up a new vista of hope and meaningfulness.

Our appreciation of silent prayer has to be touched by this anguished silence if it is fully to mature. Yet not everyone, thank God, personally knows suffering to this degree. However, some anticipation of the spiritual crisis that it might provoke is vital. Certainly a state of physical weakness and mental confusion is not itself the ideal time to allow one's prayer to develop. What we can do already is to create within ourselves a certain receptivity to the sufferings of others and to hear, with them, God's awful silence. The inner space that we make to be receptive can then become our own learning area, and ultimately our own possession of what Weil called the void. This is the practical form of prayer with which this chapter now concludes, and it is extraordinarily simple: just to listen to the one next to you who is in some pain. As we become drawn into their story and empathize with their experience, our concentrated listening may turn into a very real prayer as it enables us to encounter God anew.

Although it is simple just to listen, to listen with full attention is not always so easy, and requires a range of micro-skills. Consciously making the effort to learn these will not only enable us to be more helpful to those around us, but will also lead to a deepening of our spiritual sensitivity to God. Michael Jacobs's book, *Swift to Hear*,[10] is a useful guide. In it he tabulates seven cardinal rules for good listening:

1. Listen with undivided attention, without interrupting.
2. Remember what has been said, including the details (the more you listen and the less you say, the better your memory).
3. Listen to the 'bass line' – what is not openly said, but possibly is being felt.

4. Watch for non-verbal clues to help you understand feelings.
5. Listen to yourself, how you might feel in a described situation, as a way of further understanding – empathy.
6. Try to tolerate pauses and silences that are a little longer than is usual in conversations (and avoid asking lots of questions to break silences).
7. Help yourself and the other to feel comfortable and relaxed with each other; keep calm even when you don't feel calm.

An eighth rule for us will be to sensitize our ear to God as well as to the other person, to search for the meaning of *his* silence.

It has been well said that 'to listen another's soul into a condition of disclosure and discovery may be almost the greatest service that any human being ever performs for another'.[11] Yet we usually fail to listen with undivided attention in a thoroughly empathetic manner. It is a surprisingly demanding commitment and calls for a long and subtle learning process. But the world needs more 'good listeners'. And to do this is to begin to share in God's own mysterious self-emptying involvement with us at the very heart of human living.

Notes

1 E. Wiesel, *Night*. Harmondsworth, Penguin, 1987, p. 43.
2 See, for example, J. Hick, *Evil and the God of Love*. London, Fontana, 1968.
3 H. Küng, *Does God Exist?* London, Collins, 1980, p. 628.
4 F. Dostoevsky, *The Brothers Karamazov*. Harmondsworth, Penguin, 1958, p. 287.
5 Written from Tegel, 16 July 1944. D. Bonhoeffer, *Letters and Papers from Prison*. London, SCM, 1974, p. 360.
6 See H. Waddell, *Peter Abelard*. London, Constable, 1933.
  F. Copleston, *A History of Philosophy*, II. New York, Doubleday, 1950.
7 J. Moltmann, *The Crucified God*. London, SCM, 1974, p.276.
8 S. Weil, *Waiting on God*. London, Collins, 1959, p. 82.
9 S. Weil, *Gravity and Grace*. London, Routledge & Kegan Paul, 1952, p. 11.
10 M. Jacobs, *Swift to Hear*, New Library of Pastoral Care. London, SPCK, 1985, p. 13.
11 Referred to by the Reverend F. Longbottom, chaplain of Highcroft Hospital, Birmingham, in *A Handbook on Hospital Chaplaincy*, Hospital Chaplaincies Council. Westminster, Church House, 1987.

6 · *Peace Passing Understanding*

An attempt to describe the discovery of God in silence is bound to be inconclusive. All one can do is to sketch out the ground rules for such an encounter and recognize that it is entirely open-ended. One has to enter into the dynamics of the engagement for oneself. Having now suggested that silence may be one medium in which to find God; and having sketched out the need quietly to assimilate a framework of beliefs to use as the tools of interpretation; having faced the obliqueness of the meaning of this silence and sometimes its desperate emptiness; we come now to consider its structural significance. Sensing the reality of God for oneself may be compared with the experience of falling in love. A romance involves personal sensations of the highest and most delightful kind, but these are not usually enjoyed for their own sake. Wonderful as they are (though of course there might be an element of tragedy too), most importantly they indicate the establishment of an intense reciprocal relationship. The first feelings of love are ephemeral as the initial excitement becomes transposed into a profound commitment. To have a romance is to be led into the structure of a personal relationship. This framework then gathers its own momentum of growth as engagement leads to marriage, and marriage leads to the birth of children who themselves perhaps one day fall in love. In contemporary times it is all too obvious that a full marriage relationship cannot be sustained on the immature flutterings of romance and physical attraction. Such feelings, which do not feed into a more concrete structure of intimacy, will be inconsequential.

In a similar way, strong feelings about the presence of God have, *in themselves*, no abiding significance. What really matters is the growth of that structure of which they are merely the indicators. The growth occurs covertly and, if it is difficult to describe the exact nature of a marriage relationship, being 'a holy mystery in which man and woman become one flesh', then so much the more this spiritual structure. It remains largely hidden from view and is just not readily susceptible to objective description. But we can *begin* to say what sort of thing it is, and the historian, Arnold Toynbee, started at the right place when he described religion as essentially 'the overcoming of self-centredness, in both individuals and communities, by getting into communion with the spiritual presence behind the universe and by bringing our wills into harmony with it'.[1]

As we slowly grow to understand ourselves better, and this world in which we live; as we learn to appreciate a contemplative silence and cultivate a spiritual awareness, this structural reality emerges. The self comes to acknowledge its actual place within a wider pattern, 'the spiritual presence behind the universe'. Self-centredness is overcome by way of 'getting into communion with', and 'bringing our wills into harmony with', this greater reality. For the Christian, this is what is meant by entering into a loving relationship with the Father through baptism in Christ. The key term is integration. Rather than insisting that everything revolves around the ego, the ego (both of individuals and of communities) liberates itself to become integrated with the Divine reality.

The overcoming of self-centredness has not exactly been a primary concern in British political life during these closing decades of the twentieth century. Insistence on giving full rein to a free-market economy has led to the accumulation of private wealth being prized more highly than the excellence of such public responsibilities as state education or national health care. Integration with any greater pattern seems far from our thoughts as we concentrate on the priority of house ownership, faster travel and ever-more sophisticated leisure facilities. And yet it is in this same period that such interest has been roused in the environmental lobby. It is as if, deep down, a little voice tells us that the egocentrism which is displayed in our rampant consumerism can in the end have only one conclusion. Is it merely enlightened self-interest at work when we worry about holes in the ozone layer, or is it a resurgence of the knowledge that there is no way in which we can ultimately live only for ourselves? Environmentalists stress that we should understand ourselves to be *part of* the natural world rather than predatorial tyrants; and as the basis for this view is explained, the word 'spiritual' comes into play. The Introduction to the Green Party manifesto, for example, begins to point to an attitude of mind that goes far deeper than an interest in the recycling of paper and the abolition of lead in petrol:

Our policies – all of them – acknowledge the vital importance of our *whole* environment. That environment – its health, its safety, its *wholeness* – affects our lives, our politics, and our future, and whenever we damage the environment, we damage ourselves. Like all other forms of life, we depend for our survival and wellbeing upon a fragile network of physical, social and spiritual links with the rest of creation.... We need to recognize the spiritual dimension of our lives, just as we need food to eat and friends to love.[2]

Moreover, it may be that the 'spiritual dimension of our lives' is somewhat more than is suggested by the description of a 'fragile network of ... links with the rest of creation'. The appreciation of silence alerts us to a presence – loving, steady – a reality somehow worthy of our deepest response. It is easy to think of 'creation' as an enclosed system, but contemplation opens us to the inexhaustible mystery at the heart of this network. The Green movement emphasizes the need for integration, and goes as far as to use the word spiritual. Another contemporary social phenomenon pursues more explicitly the priority of spiritual awareness. This is the current wave of interest in exotic religions, cults and beliefs, often pejoratively named as the 'occult'. In his book, *Inner Visions*, [3] Nevill Drury more helpfully notes the broad base of this interest and renames it the 'consciousness movement'. Drury sees the phenomenon as a collective realization of our alienation from the world, and as an attempt to restore ourselves by recapturing a sense of magic and mystery. 'Despite the growth of a vastly complex mechanistic environment in our urban sprawl, certain philosophies of reaction have emerged.' 'The consciousness movement seems to be asking collectively: what is the fullest span of perception accessible to man; what is his most deeply felt sense of reality and of what does it consist?' Drury's curiously eclectic study ranges from tarot cards and the cabbala, surrealist art and modern psychology, to rock music. Hard as it often is to take the material he examines wholly seriously, he nevertheless tenders a valuable explanation for the current interest in such things. He believes that we are witnessing a new 'ecology of the mind' in which the desire for self-awareness is being allied to anxieties about the physical environment – out of which a renewed cosmology will finally emerge:

It would be easy enough to dismiss the present trends of the counter-culture if it were not for the fact that its cumulative direction does seem to point to a deeply felt need for belief systems which allow a sense of identification with the earth, the environment and the forces of nature.... We are living in interesting times – an era in fact which may well see major transformations in the consensus reality.[4]

In the midst of our self-seeking culture then, with its myriad of conflicting sectional interests, there are those who recognize the bankruptcy of egocentrism. The Green movement urges us to see that we are but a part of a wider natural order. The 'consciousness movement' calls us to search for a new spiritual harmony. Both are expressive of what I suggest is a fundamental human need: the desire to be thoroughly integrated with the fullness of reality. Who knows but that many might not feel an urgent dissatisfaction with closed human systems of thought and behaviour if there is indeed an Ultimate to develop our relatedness with? Jesus spoke of a great treasure buried in a field, and of a certain merchant who, when he found it, sold all he had and bought that field (Matt. 13.44). The structure of participation with God is that treasure, hidden and buried below the surface of much conscious activity, but of inestimable value. An appreciation of silence and the practice of contemplation, as we enter therein, begins to effect exactly this transcendence of egoism and integration of self with the Divine.

What matters most is the establishment of this hidden structure, then, and this will be confirmed if we now re-examine the nature of our personal experiences of God. Back in Chapter 1, three conversations with some very ordinary people were referred to. It seems to me that all three were aware of being drawn into a deeper form of life which was somehow a continuum lying beneath the surface realities of a day-to-day existence. They politely described their various religious experiences to me, but I felt that what they were able to put into words was profoundly dissatisfying to them in that it failed to capture the occurrence of some almost organic growth which the experiences betokened. What they talked about was merely the froth on top. Not so easy to describe was the sense of having responded (or at least having recognized the possibility of responding) to an invitation to enter into a new, secret and inexhaustible structure of being. Mrs T spoke of 'a being of some kind . . . that takes hold of us in certain ways'. I might have asked her how she felt she had been taken hold of. However, perhaps the most important thing for me to know was that there were moments when she felt that she was not simply a solitary individual wandering through life, but one who *had* been taken hold of and whose life was being woven into an eternal pattern.

The Reverend E described an intensely peaceful moment experienced in a wine cellar while on holiday in France. He said he felt in that moment 'deeply good, a rested, peaceful feeling' and it sounded as though he had been spontaneously immersed in a sense of being in tune with his surroundings. I connected this moment with his earlier admission that he tended to conceive of God as 'deep within me', 'the ground of my being', and surmised that what he felt was actually being in tune with God. Mrs T then used this sort of language much more explicitly. She spoke of God as One with whom she was wholly wrapped up. She did not feel that she possessed any clear image of God to describe for me, 'no great light shining, no vision of God'. But what came across was the discovery that her own personal life was in fact located in the Divine context. 'I just feel that there *is* something which really does affect us all – in different ways because we are different personalities.' Reflecting on their comments, I came away with the conviction that these people, whose experiences are after all not so extraordinary, have begun to be rooted and grounded in a reality that exceeds their own being. None of them were particularly interested in mysticism as such; they could hardly be said to have lost themselves in some religious obsession. On the contrary, they seemed to me to have found their identity within a new framework of security and meaning.

According to the Prayer Book Catechism, as alluded to earlier, the sacraments have been granted to us as a pledge of God's grace and as a means to receive the same. The sacramental body and blood of Christ strengthens and refreshes our souls; it brings us to salvation. So when we receive Holy Communion we pray that our participation in God will thereby be revived and renewed. The Prayer Book rite concludes with a prayer of thanksgiving, 'for that thou dost vouchsafe to feed us, who have duly received these holy mysteries . . . and that we are very members incorporate in the mystical body of thy Son, which is the blessed company of all faithful people'. If silence is a natural sacrament of God, then we should not be surprised if it too enables us to grow as members incorporate in the mystical body.

Keeping silence, we are slowly integrated with the One who is silently present to us. Liturgical language talks about the Eucharistic bread and wine nourishing us, and in a similar way silence can feed the organic growth of our structural interaction with the Divine.

The view that something concrete is being established by way of particular religious experiences, which in that sense lies below the surface of what is reported, can be illustrated by reference to some of the material produced by the Religious Experience Research Unit at Manchester College, Oxford. In his book, *This Time-Bound Ladder*, the researcher Edward Robinson relates various conversations held at his supper table. He asked the Orthodox priest, Archimandrite Lev Gillet, to characterize a personal religious phenomenon: 'Firstly, the awareness of a reality which transcends you: something bigger than yourself, something beyond your own limits. And secondly, although it is transcendent, it must in some way be immanent to yourself, you must find it in yourself.' Having used a perceptual language of awareness and discovery, Gillet then mentioned the building up of a reciprocal interchange with the One encountered, and this somehow sounds to be more the *substance* of the experience: 'And thirdly, between these two expressions of a supreme reality . . . there is a possibility of dynamic exchange. You receive something from it, and you give something to it.'[5] Martin Israel, Anglican priest and senior lecturer in pathology at the University of London, used the notion of integration more explicitly when it was his turn, as the coffee arrived, to describe religious experience:

> I would say that religious experience is an experience of that which transcends the individual and makes him a fuller individual, which makes the personality more integrated in terms of under-standing his place in the world; an experience that there is something outside him, of which he has been made aware, that broadens his view of life, something that gives him a widened awareness, and brings him to thoughts of Deity.[6]

Thus both Gillet and Israel envisage an encounter with a Reality greater than oneself, but imply that a participation with this Reality creates an enhanced self-identity. We should not ever expect such a state of self-integration with the Divine to be referred to in any dispassionate manner. The experiences that manifest the state are characterized on the one hand by the conviction that something objectively real has been encountered; and on the other hand, by a totally subjective widening of self-awareness. As Gillet said, 'You receive something from it, and you give something to it.' Another dinner guest, the writer and journalist Monica Furlong, emphasized the personal value of the structure underlying religious experience. For her there is an assurance that 'on the far side of all the most frightful ups and downs one is constantly experiencing there is something else – that one can hold on to'.[7] This is a refreshingly pragmatic appreciation. We may enjoy speculating about the nature of the structure, but the most important function of any structure is to provide security!

This, then, is the hidden structure being established when we keep silence with God; the integration into which we secretly enter through our contemplation. As we develop this understanding, it might be tempting to suppose that the silence itself, the actual medium of the experience, is merely superficial and does not matter. This is not so. The medium, whether it be a religious sacrament, silence, or some other feature of the natural world, is not dispensable. In her table-talk, Rosalind Heywood noted that her spiritual experience was always prompted by some particular stimulus:

> I never seem to have any of this sort of experience unless it's to do with other people or with – I think the only word I can use is beauty. It may be beauty on a mountain, or on the sea, in a cathedral or where you will. Beauty will get me out of myself; it's as if beauty were one of the absolutes. It's difficult to put into words but I think that it makes you entirely forget your little ego, which seems to me the first step towards real awareness of anything else.[8]

If silence is the medium of the experience, then it too becomes an absolute: we cannot separate the medium from the message, the silence from the One of whom it is sacramental.

So we leave Mr Robinson's dinner table with some corroboration of the view that the structure that an appreciation of silence helps us to enter is one in which 'your life is hid with Christ in God' (Col. 3.3). These conversations also confirm the odd feeling that integration comes to us *from* God, and not the other way about. We are drawn into a greater Reality, woven into a wider pattern, and there we find ourselves. Lev Gillet described this as 'the method of infiltration by God'. He alluded to the story in Luke's Gospel of the journey to Emmaus, noting that in this case Jesus did not confront the two disciples, but approached them from behind. 'He follows them, listens to them, and hears them, and enters into their talk. This is not the way of speaking with authority, but the method of infiltration. He can enter us as ink can penetrate blotting paper.'[9] This reminds us of the priority of silence simply as receptivity.

If now we turn to examine how one of the great classical guides to the spiritual life described the development of mystical experience, we shall be able to build up a more detailed understanding of its underlying structure. St John of the Cross (1542–91) was watered at the fountain of that rather heady spirituality produced in sixteenth-century Catholic Spain. Becoming a Carmelite monk at the age of twenty-one, he soon became dissatisfied with what he felt to be its laxity. St Teresa of Avila was already leading a reform among the women, and John supported this movement towards greater austerity. For St John of the Cross, the goal of the spiritual life was union with God, a profound state of being; he interpreted that which was commonly experienced as so many stages in this process of development. In many ways, John spoke a language very alien to the Christians of our day. He seems to us both excessively florid, addressing Christ in an overtly sensual manner as the 'bridegroom of the soul'; and also harshly austere, we do not quite know what to make of his mental and physical mortifications. Nevertheless, the writings of St John of the Cross are again curiously popular in our day. Perhaps the common ground is a preoccupation with experience. The modern fascination with self-knowledge and awareness connects with John's world of colourful meditations and visions. He helps us to place today's experience in the broader context of our growth towards God. He provides us with a map of our spiritual journey so that we can know the structure into which we are entering from the standpoint of what we are currently experiencing.

When we say that we are looking for an integration of ourselves with the greater reality of God, then St John of the Cross speaks more explicitly of the soul's ecstatic union with God: 'The soul is immersed in God, it surrenders itself, most willingly and with great sweetness, to Him wholly, desiring to be wholly His and never again to have aught in itself that is alien from Him'.[10] In such passages we may feel that John is really describing something quite different to our experience. Our modest intimations of, and reachings out towards, God hardly seem to correspond to his sense of passionate possession by the Divine Lover. We must of course have the humility to acknowledge that John had opened himself to God to an extent greater than most of us will ever allow ourselves to be. (Indeed, one can observe a contemporary disinclination to believe oneself spiritually inferior to anyone else!) And we must allow for his florid Counter-Reformation style of spirituality, of which devotion to a very physical image of Christ with the language of human intimacy was characteristic. But, after such qualifications, the writings of St John of the Cross emerge as a magisterial treatment of the undergirding structure of the spiritual life. Despite the culture-gap, they still represent an important authority for us today.

To hear what St John of the Cross has to say about (what we have begun to call) the state of integration with God, we might best turn to his poetry. The poem 'Songs of the soul in rapture'[11] forms the basis of his book, *The Ascent of Mount Carmel*, which is a commentary on it. If now we ask, 'What does it mean to be integrated with God?', this poem will paint for us its main attributes. And at once we are in the realm of silent contemplation. The first stanzas express the hush and stillness that bear us to the point of meeting:

> Upon a gloomy night,
> With all my cares to loving ardours flushed,
> (O venture of delight!)
> With nobody in sight
> I went abroad when all my house was hushed.

> In safety, in disguise,
> In darkness up the secret stair I crept,
> (O happy enterprise)
> Concealed from other eyes
> When all my house at length in silence slept.

Then there is a curious ambivalence about the loving presence of God which the soul seeks so eagerly. The encounter is cloaked in darkness, and although the soul has an interior light to guide her to him, yet he waits hidden in the shadows:

> Upon that lucky night
> In secrecy, inscrutable to sight,
> I went without discerning
> And with no other light
> Except for that which in my heart was burning.

It lit and led me through
More certain than the light of noonday clear
To where One waited near
Whose presence well I knew,
There where no other presence might appear.

Clearly, a love tryst has been entered into and the meeting prearranged.
So we begin to feel the force of the mutuality of the exchange. God
waits longingly for the soul who goes ardently to the secret place.
There is a dynamic of attraction and romantic irresistibility:

Oh night that was my guide!
Oh darkness dearer than the morning's pride,
Oh night that joined the lover
To the beloved bride
Transfiguring them into each other.

Within my flowering breast
Which only for himself entire I save
He sank into his rest
And all my gifts I gave
Lulled by the airs with which the cedars wave.

Now the extraordinarily explicit sensual imagery begins to express
the utter joy and abandonment and total happiness. Yet at the same
time there is something irreducibly *strange* about the whole affair.
The Lover remains a mysterious figure and he seems to exert an
almost fearsome power over the soul. The climax of ecstasy with
which the poem concludes leaves us with the impression that this is
quite unique and without compare. The human yearning for love has
been entirely, and for ever, satisfied:

Over the ramparts fanned
While the fresh wind was fluttering his tresses,
With his serenest hand
My neck he wounded, and
Suspended every sense with its caresses.

Lost to myself I stayed
My face upon my lover having laid
From all endeavour ceasing:
And all my cares releasing
Threw them amongst the lillies there to fade.

Thus the poem begins and ends in silence; the soul moves from the hush in which she sets out for the Lover through to the joyful acquiescence of her final abandonment. The erotic imagery may not be quite our cup of tea, but if we extract the poem's essential meaning we shall have in our hands a concrete definition of that state with God to which our silence leads us. It is a deeply reciprocal exchange. The One to whom we relate so profoundly nevertheless remains mysteriously hidden. There is something 'odd', in the strict meaning of the word, about this involvement, for we are the lesser responding to the greater. This state of being brings a joy and a personal satisfaction without paramour. The establishment of this structure is *the reason* for learning to appreciate silence and to practise contemplation. For Christians, its cultivation must be *the one priority*: the treasure found buried in a field. For us this identifies, so far as it can be identified, that fuller integration – a yearning for which is never far below the surface of any society.

Is it really Christian, though? Are we attempting to substitute a vague, wishy-washy mysticism for the revelation of God in Christ through the power of his Holy Spirit? Since here we are developing an appreciation of silence from a Christian perspective, and since we have agreed that spiritual experience necessarily involves the assimilation of particular doctrines which can then be used interpretatively, the integrity of our study requires us to remain true to our Christian identity. In the first place, then, we may wonder what significance the cross of Christ has in relation to the state of integration. Or are we able to circumvent pain and sacrifice by enabling an immediate access to the consolations of God? Here we return for guidance to St John of the Cross. If we read him carefully, we shall soon discover that the ecstatic joy which he describes in his poetry is but the goal of a long and arduous pilgrimage. He does not mince his words: 'so great are the trials, and so profound the darkness, spiritual as well as corporal through which souls must pass, if they will attain to perfection, that no human learning can explain them, nor experience describe them'.[12]

The passion of Christ speaks to us of that mode of being which alone will bring us to God. 'And he said to all, "If any man would come after me, let him deny himself and take up his cross daily and follow me. For whoever would save his life will lose it; and whoever loses his life for my sake, he will save it"' (Luke 9.23). St John of the Cross leaves us in no doubt that the prerequisite for spiritual

growth is indeed a readiness to lose, as it were, one's very life. We
are to follow a way of renunciation. In the first place John urges a
detachment from all that we enjoy on a merely physical plane; we are
to love the Creator rather than his creatures. Now it may sound as if
John is making a monkish distinction between the world and things
of the spirit, whereas our approach has been to view elements of the
natural world as sacramental of God. But what he really says is that
we should not use material things as if they were ends in themselves;
'It is not the things of this world that occupy or injure the soul, for
they do not enter within, but rather the wish for, and desire of them
which abide within it.'[13] His teaching (even if he did not follow it
through himself) actually enables us to be thoroughly world-
affirming – once we learn to search for that which is the ground of its
being. But if we never move beyond satisfaction of the senses, our
spiritual sensibilities will remain benighted: 'All the love we bestow
on creatures is in the eyes of God mere darkness, and while we are
involved therein, the soul is incapable of being enlightened and
possessed by the pure and simple light of God, unless we first cast
that love away'.[14]

This is the first sacrifice, and it follows from recognizing God as
our true end: to renounce a selfish enjoyment of material pleasures as
we come instead to appreciate them as *means* to this end. Much self-
discipline will be required and John does not spare us its harshness;
we are 'to go by a way wherein thou hast no pleasure'.[15] He quickly
dispels any thoughts that the process of integration with the Divine
Reality is a comfortable and self-satisfying mysticism. It is indeed a
Way of the Cross. We are to 'have pleasure in nothing', 'possess
nothing', 'be nothing' and 'know nothing'. 'For in order to pass
from the all to the All, thou hast to deny thyself wholly in all'. Of
course this is possible, as John makes clear, only when we have
already begun to receive 'a greater enkindling by another, and a
better love'.[16] And then this better love, as we grow and become
integrated with it, will inwardly urge us to make a renunciation even
more painful. John calls this the Dark Night of the spirit, which
must follow that of the senses.

All our human picturing and conceptualizing of God must now
cease. We are to aspire, it is implied, to a higher form of consciousness than that of reason. We shall then be open to 'truths revealed by
God Himself, which transcend all natural light, and exceed all
human understanding, beyond all proportion'.[17] Now St John of the

Cross was heir to a philosophical tradition in the light of which such claims were meaningful. We are not. It is hard for us to make sense of the implication that there is a form of knowledge more reasonable than reason. St John of the Cross seems to be suggesting that the powers of the mind must be wholly shut down if we are to apprehend God in a more authentic manner. Our intellectual self-understanding rebels at this: far from bringing us to the glories of God, it would leave us in a vegetative state of coma! Nevertheless, this is not the moment to part company with St John of the Cross. Provided we make our own contemporary reinterpretation, he will yet prove to be a reliable guide.

We discussed above the potential of silence as natural sacrament. But any sacrament involves the interpretation of data by particular beliefs. So we then discussed that silence in which overt beliefs are mulled over and digested into an implicit form. In this form they enable the act of interpretation to be made smoothly and with a minimum of self-consciousness. We agreed then that to assimilate a corpus of beliefs is, in effect, to *forget* them. That is, one remains aware of their significance, but not of the beliefs in themselves. A pianist lost in the sublime beauty of a Beethoven Sonata has no knowledge of musical theory running consciously through her mind. That theory was once painfully learnt, but then digested as it came to be applied in the development of the pianist's personal skills. St John of the Cross is wrong when he asserts that the use of our reason is to be rejected if we want to know God. Indeed, how dangerous is the thoroughly irrational religion! But he is right when he suggests that we have to move below the surface meaning of our beliefs, and that this will represent a painful loss to the conscious mind.

St John of the Cross identifies a moment in one's spiritual growth when it is right to progress from meditation to contemplation. This transition marks the work of assimilation. It occurs when our meditation becomes quieter as the beliefs about which we have been meditating slip below the horizon of our conscious ratiocinations. Their essential goodness has been extracted by much chewing and is now nourishing our spiritual understanding. John warns us not to anticipate the moment, 'not to lay aside the said imaginative meditation before the proper time lest he should turn backward'. An incomplete appreciation of our beliefs will be able to facilitate only a partial experience of that Divine Reality that they represent: 'these . . . are necessary to beginners, in order that they may gradually feed and enkindle their souls'.[18] But when the moment *does* come, we are to accept it joyfully and 'to abide attentively and wait lovingly upon God in that state of quiet'.[19]

However, entering the state of quiet will not necessarily be a congenial experience. John warns us that as we become less conscious of our ideas *about* God, so we may feel ourselves to have wholly lost our way. Prayer may seem to have become a pointless exercise: 'they think that they are going astray and wasting time'.[20] If we persist, as he urges us to, it will be to accept an increasing sense of inner emptiness and aridity. In his book, *The Dark Night of the Soul*, John admits in no uncertain terms the pain involved. 'The soul is conscious of a profound emptiness, and destitution. . . . It is like that of a person being suffocated, or hindered from breathing.'[21] But this distress is a necessary part of the process of spiritually growing up. He compares it with the transition of an infant being weaned from its mother's breasts on to solid food. At first we take comfort in overt beliefs and the natural working of our minds as we aspire to know God. We are 'spiritually nursed and caressed, as an infant by its loving mother, who warms it in her bosom, nourishes it with her own sweet milk, feeds it with tender and delicate food, carries it in her arms, and fondles it'. But our early infantile awareness of God soon leads us on towards a personal encounter with him. Then ideas about God require substituting with an actual taste of his presence. We become the growing child who needs a more substantial food, and a greater independence from its mother. So, 'the mother witholds her caresses, hides her breasts, and anoints them with the juice of bitter aloes; she carries the infant in her arms no longer, but makes it walk on the ground'.[22]

For St John of the Cross, the emptiness of mind that ensues results from the literal rejection of all human thought so that we may know God in an altogether different, mystical way. For us, it will be a relative emptiness, resulting from the thorough assimilation of beliefs which are then no longer self-consciously held in the mind. But his description of the quality of the experience is unexaggerated: aridity and bitterness, a virtual suffocation of religious sensibilities. John also points faithfully to that mysterious structure of human–Divine mutuality of which this barren silence is the access. We may feel that we have completely lost our way, while in fact this state of naked vulnerability indicates our growth from a mere religiosity towards a genuine integration with God himself. The traveller 'will never reach a new country, but by new ways which he knows not, and by abandoning those he knew – so in the same way the soul makes the greater progress when it travels in the dark, not knowing the way'.[23] It is true that we have had to make a rather drastic reinterpretation of John's emphasis on the need to renounce all human thoughts and imaginings about God. But his central emphasis remains, for we do have to renounce the use of religious beliefs as props and comforters, we have to enter into them and actually *live them* – and this will feel surprisingly like giving them up altogether. We have to step away from their all-enclosing security out into the unknown.

Those who seriously pursue the spiritual implications of ecology politics, recognizing the need for a sense of affinity with the environment; those affected by the consciousness movement who look both within and around at a world of which they are part; these of our contemporaries who distinctively signal a more universally felt imperative to discover full meaning in an integration with that beyond themselves must at some point face this silence. Ideas *about* integration merely massage the ego. Instead, we have to follow the example of that Man who, rather than just meditating deeply about the nature of love, chose *to love* – and to the utter limits; far from merely preaching about the way to God, in a total giving of himself he became the way. In no sense can our silent contemplation circumvent the centrality of that cross. Thus St John of the Cross spells out some home truths which, in a society whose popular spirituality sometimes seems to be dangerously close to plain self-interest, need to be heard loud and clear. That peace and quiet in which the presence of God may first be sensed has to be followed through into a hard silence which is nothing less than an exposure of the self and an acceptance of emptiness.

At no time was this made clearer than in the case of the first Christian monks who fled from the cities of fourth-century civilization into the desert area of the Nile delta. The complete explanation of this strange social phenomenon is no doubt complex, but the primary motivation of these Desert Fathers was simple: to seek God, and in the search for him to set everything else to one side. They chose the desert as an appropriate place in which to conduct this search, because it was so totally empty and free from all secondary distractions. The contemporary Rufinus describes it: 'There is a huge silence and a great quiet there.'[24] The collected 'Sayings' of the Desert Fathers seem to have quite a popular appeal today, and perhaps this is because we too yearn for a *quies magna*, a great quiet, in which God can be met. I wonder, though, if we are ready for the absolute self-exposure that these early monks embraced in the huge silence of the desert? We hear, for example, of an older man to whom a younger brother came and asked, 'How can I be saved?' With typical economy of speech, the monk simply removed his clothes and then said that this was how one had to become, naked before God.[25]

At first the brothers spent much of their time alone in their cells, reciting the psalms, eating a frugal diet, coming together occasionally for the Eucharist. Rufinus continued his description, 'They inhabit a desert place and have their cells some distance from each other, so that no one should be recognized from afar by another, or hear another's voice. On the contrary, they live in profound silence, each monk isolated on his own.'[26] This silence constantly reminded them of the reason for their being there, and of the One whom they sought. They concentrated on this work, to which we hear Abbot Moses recalling one brother in his ringing words, 'Go, sit in your cell, and your cell will teach you everything.'[27] However, the brothers soon discovered that far from being a refuge from all desires that conflicted with the search for God, the desert raised up such temptations even more powerfully. Erotic dreams, visions of demons, feelings of jealousy and unforgiveness towards their fellow monks: such things assumed a greater intensity and irresistibility in the *quies magna*. The desert was not a refuge, but it did become a battlefield. If the self was exposed, then so were its enemies, and the struggle could be engaged in deadly earnest. We have here already uncovered this harsh reality of contemplative silence. In it, we meet ourselves and this meeting may be highly disturbing. Yet the struggle with all that keeps us centred in the self is a necessary one. Only so will we ever be able to hand ourselves over to God.

They did not like to talk about it, but what sustained this desert enterprise was the fact that its silence evidently did bring some of the brothers into a wonderful intimacy with God. Rufinus, for example, relates a notable sermon preached by John of Lycopolis:

> If we stand before God with a pure heart ... we can, insofar as this is possible, see even God, and as we pray the eyes of our heart are turned towards him and we see that which is invisible. ... If then he will know ... the mysteries of God, and insofar as his mind

becomes more pure. . . . He will become the friend of God . . . and whatever he asks, God will grant it to him, as to a dear friend.[28]

Those who became able to receive this friendship with God spoke of *apatheia*, natural human desires being held in perfect balance; and of *hesycheia*, an inner stillness and serenity. Those who achieved this state of integration with the Divine reminded the army of other monks still battling away just what the point of remaining with the silence was. They surely could not help but see, in the eyes of the few, the treasure that was there to be received. But the most notable characteristic of those who had become 'friends of God' was their extreme reluctance to verbalize the experience. No doubt there was the fear of falling into pride and vanity, of thinking themselves a cut above their brothers. But there seems also to have been the realization that the structure that had evolved in the silence was somehow mysterious, profound, and not to be trivialized in limited human speech. A group of visitors came to one such monk named Bes and described the meeting: 'He lived a life of the utmost stillness, and his manner was serene. . . . He was extremely humble and held himself of no account. We pressed him to speak a word of encouragement to us, but he only consented to say a little about meekness, and was reluctant to do even that.'[29] Being intimate with God there was, in a sense, nothing more to be said.

Theologians have never found it easy to define this communion with God which is the hidden reality which grows as one progresses in the spiritual life. And in our own day we are often most ill at ease with that which cannot be defined. Yet for all of us who admit to any sense of spiritual awareness, there are moments when we feel ourselves to have become involved in a Reality that is the ground of our reality, and which is, for this very reason, beyond a properly objective description. Eastern Christianity has done most to develop an understanding of the manner in which we are able to participate in God the supreme mystery. The second-century bishop, St Irenaeus, articulated the key idea with his oft-repeated phrase, 'God became man in order that man might become God'. On this basis, silent prayer has come to have a central place in the spirituality of the Eastern Church, with its emphasis on the belief that our highest vocation is not merely to know and address God, but actually to participate in him. So we find the fifth-century St Mark the Hermit saying that as we do this we will, in a sense, take on the

Divine image: 'The spirit receives into itself the characteristics of a deiform image, and becomes clothed with the ineffable beauty of the likeness of the Lord.'[30] But then it has seemed to other Christians that to speak of the deification of humanity is to topple into absurdity. Surely it is obfuscating to imply that we could ever *take on* elements of the Divine nature? Would it not be better to say simply that a high degree of intimacy with God is possible, and that in a wonderfully reciprocal manner? And yet in saying this we are doing little more than passing on the invitation from God. In the end we must simply *be silent*, and allow ourselves to be drawn into this beautiful structure of human being.

A sense of the 'otherness' of God, and of the deep mutuality that this provokes, are essential characteristics of that secret structure which is the concrete reality of all authentic personal spirituality. Yet however convinced we become about its objective reality, it always sounds as if we are merely speaking about our own intense subjective feelings. Now if our religion rests on personal experience (and I find it impossible to comprehend any religion that does not), this will represent a continuous and inevitable dilemma. How to separate the reality of God from my subjective circumstances and from my deepest psychological needs? While as Christians we insist that in principle this must be possible, I suspect that in practice it is not. The psychologist C. G. Jung rediscovered God in his study of the human mind, and I find his basic admission liberating: 'It is only through the psyche that we can establish that God acts upon us, but we are unable to distinguish whether God and the unconscious are two different entities.' If this is the case, then we should not have any guilt in articulating our spirituality in terms of our personal condition. So, while the structure that undergirds religious experience is an actual integration of the self with the Divine, we shall inevitably have to speak about a condition of *self-integration*. Jung goes on to confirm my suggestion that to find God is to begin to achieve self-integration, for 'there is in the unconscious an archetype of wholeness . . . and a tendency . . . to relate other archetypes to this centre'. 'It is this archetype from whch we can no longer distinguish the God-image empirically.'[31]

If the quest for religious experience requires any justification, then we have it here. What could be more important to anyone than the achievement of personal integration? And if this sounds unduly selfish, then we must know that we cannot fully love another before we have found ourselves; the self must be gathered together before it can be sacrificed. Jung stresses the inestimable value of integration in noting that it is a pure, absolute state which cannot be compared with anything else. 'It can only be experienced. It is a subjective affair quite beyond discussion; we have a particular feeling about ourselves, about the way we are, and that is a fact which is neither possible nor meaningful to doubt.' [32]This is *it*. *This* is that treasure found buried in a field for which we all search. In one of the most moving passages of his writings, Jung came finally to name this central reality as Love – and then, God:

> Being a part, man cannot see the whole. He is at its mercy. He may assent to it, or rebel against it; but he is always caught up by it and enclosed within it. He is dependent upon it and is sustained by it . . . . Man can try to name love, showering upon it all the names at his command, and still he will involve himself in endless self-deceptions. If he possesses a grain of wisdom, he will lay down his arms and name the unknown by the more unknown, *ignotum per ignotus* – that is, by the name of God.[33]

Personal meaning (the means to achieve which Jung struggled so long to understand) comes when we are caught up by, enclosed within, dependent upon and sustained by – that is, thoroughly integrated with – God.

Various forms of prayer have been suggested for the reader to practise in the light of the different aspects of silence that we have discovered. We began with some evidence that silence is sometimes the medium in which people first become aware of the presence of God. It was suggested that we could do worse than follow the advice of Brother Lawrence, and address in simple words the One with whom contact has been made, 'Father . . .'. We then concentrated on the nature of this medium and realized that it functioned in a sacramental way. To develop this understanding, we went to pray before the reserved Eucharistic bread, thinking to ourselves that just as that bread communicates the real presence of Christ, so silence can communicate the Divine presence. Then we looked at the role of formal beliefs, and saw that personal experience depends always on our tacit use of them. The ancient art of *lectio divina* was proposed as a helpful means by which to 'read, mark, learn and inwardly digest'. A very physical form of prayer was next suggested, right posture and right breathing, in which mind and body control themselves and learn to wait for God. Then in the last chapter, touching the depths of human suffering, it was suggested that the act of simply listening fully to others in the outpourings of their hearts could become a form of personal prayer. Our attending to silence has not been a wholly comfortable affair. Nor will it be. Certainly we may hope to find in the silence of contemplation, peace, serenity, a touch of God's presence and an overbrimming joy. But we shall also undoubtedly find there our partial ideas and beliefs exposed to doubt and contradiction. We shall be faced with the deafening silence of God's outrageous absence as his innocent children are tortured and killed. In the emptiness, our private despair and sense of meaninglessness will be free to well up within ourselves. Silent prayer is certainly not the easy twentieth-century option for those who want an instant spirituality.

Nevertheless, in this chapter we have dealt most positively on that structure of integration with the Divine that is the hidden reality undergirding all the different stages, good and bad, of our spiritual formation. An appropriate form of prayer now will be one in which we can capture, albeit briefly, something of the joy, fullness of being, and harmony of such an integration. Unfortunately, we cannot arrange prayer like this, but only be ready to welcome it when it comes. For much of the time prayer is a hard slog – remember those long afternoons Father Hollings spent as a seminarian in Rome? But if we are patient, there will be moments when the heavens suddenly open and we are flooded with the most sublime feelings. This is the prayer of joyful wonder when it seems that we are spontaneously wrapped up in God. The silence then conveys a plenitude of meaning and we seem to have a profound inner stillness.

Eastern Christianity has somehow managed to incorporate the possibility of this sort of awareness of God, this inner stillness, into the heart of its liturgy and corporate life. So St Gregory of Sinai writes of a 'wonder' which is 'a total transport of the soul towards what is discerned of the wondrous glory of the Deity, ... a pure and entire stretching of the mind outwards towards the limitless power of the light'. [34] To capture this sense of joyfulness, this prayer of wonder, we need only to still the heart. Ironically, this may happen to us in a spontaneous unplanned manner, when the sense of wonder is quite unlooked for, and then it may recur again only after many years of hard and patient prayer. 'For beginners', says St Gregory, 'prayer is like a joyous flame bursting out of the heart; and for the perfect it is like a sweet-scented light acting within it'. It is silly to pretend that we do not need this awareness and to say that we should rely on pure faith. Only the angels can do that! But we *should* come to appreciate its deeper significance, which is that it indicates the growth of that wonderful structural reality in which we are, truly, growing together with God. Silence in what St Gregory calls the 'sanctuary of the spirit' prepares us for more than we presently know:

> ... the Sanctuary of the spirit is the mysterious mental perform-
> ing of mind on the altar of the soul, both officiating and partaking
> of the Lamb, in betrothal with God. To eat of the Lamb on the
> mental altar of the soul means not only to know it, or to partake of
> it, but in the future to be like as the Lamb, fashioned in its own
> image. Here we have only the words, but there we hope to receive
> the very substance of the mysteries.[35]

Notes

1 A. Toynbee, *Surviving the Future*. Oxford, Oxford University Press, 1971, p. 66.
2 From the Introduction to the *Green Party Manifesto*. London, Heretic Books, GMP Publishers Ltd, 1987, p. 1.
3 N. Drury, *Inner Visions: Exploration in Magical Consciousness*. London, Routledge & Kegan Paul, 1979, pp. 2–3.
4 ibid., p. 125.
5 E. Robinson, *This Time-Bound Ladder*. The Religious Experience Research Unit, Manchester College, Oxford, 1977, pp. 29–30.
6 ibid., p. 48.
7 ibid., p. 101.
8 ibid., p. 63.
9 ibid., p. 46.
10 John of the Cross, *The Spiritual Canticle*, trans. E. Allison Peers. London, Burns & Oates, 1978, stanza XVII.4., p. 109.
11 John of the Cross, 'Songs of the soul in rapture ... ', in *Poems of St John of the Cross*, trans. R. Campbell. London, Harvill Press, 1951, pp. 11–13.
12 John of the Cross, *The Ascent of Mount Carmel*, trans. E. Allison Peers. London, Burns & Oates, 1983, Prologue 1.
13 ibid., I.III.4.
14 ibid., I.IV.1.
15 ibid., I.XIII.
16 ibid., I.XIV.2.
17 ibid., II.III.1.
18 ibid., II.XII.5.

19 ibid., II.XII.8.
20 ibid., II.XIV.4.
21 John of the Cross, *The Dark Night of the Soul*, trans. B. Zimmerman. Cambridge, James Clarke & Co., 1973, II.VI.6.
22 ibid., I.I.2.
23 ibid., II.XVI.9.
24 *The Lives of the Desert Fathers*, trans. B. Ward. London and Oxford, Mowbray, 1981, p. 3.
25 ibid., p. 34.
26 ibid., p. 106.
27 *The Wisdom of the Desert*, trans. T. Merton, London, Sheldon Press, 1974, p. 30.
28 *The Lives of the Desert Fathers*, p. 146.
29 ibid., p. 66.
30 See V. Lossky, *The Mystical Theology of the Eastern Church*. Cambridge, James Clarke & Co, 1957, p. 212.
31 C. G. Jung, *Memories, Dreams and Reflections*. London, Fontana, 1983, p. 413.
32 ibid., p. 317.
33 ibid., p. 387.
34 *Writings from the Philocalia*, trans. E. Kadloubovsky and G. E. H. Palmer. London, Faber & Faber, 1951, p. 47.
35 ibid., p. 48.

7 · Impregnated with Silence

Hush, be still; welcome!
Older than the mountains, purer than the sky.
In the beginning: silence.
We cover you over and hide from you.
But you are here, always, for us;
you – silence – You.

Silence is a primordial quality. Scientists speculate that before the big bang that marked the beginning of the universe, there existed a centre of intense mass and energy. Our minds imagine a surrounding environment of utter emptiness. Christian thinkers have reasoned even more fundamentally that God created the world *ex nihilo*, out of nothing. Thus 'older than the mountains' must be the silence of this primordial *nihilo*. Both the scientist and the theologian might say that we, and the whole natural world, have emerged out of silence. Others will continue – though not the Christian – by saying that in death we return to a total silence. But to us all the underlying existence of this primordial *nihilo* may seem frightening, threatening to crush our vulnerable human forms. Nevertheless, I have tried to suggest that silence is actually a medium in which we may come to experience God. But in doing this I have not wanted to pretend that silence is always comfortable and positive. It seems to me that often it is frightening. Silence has an unknown depth. The apparent loss of form and language easily makes us panic, for our feet can no longer feel the bottom, and we fear that we will drown in a gulf of meaninglessness. It is not surprising that we instinctively tend to cover over silence and hide from it. However, if God can be described as the ground of our being, it may be in silence that we are able to come closest to that primordial source of all life.

So it is that we may find silence to have purity, a special transparency of God, which it is simply self-diminishing for us to deny. Silence allows us access to a form of experience which, far from being merely an esoteric concern for the mystically inclined, is fundamental to what it means to be human. Silence puts us in touch with that from which we have emerged, that in which (however unknowingly) we are rooted.

In my work as chaplain to an independent hospital, which happens to be in a quiet rural setting, I am struck by the large number of patients who undertake a review of their attitudes and priorities while they are there. Being temporarily lifted out of the relentless round of busy-ness creates a space in which both the experience of illness and the beauty of the surrounding countryside then prompt some deep thought. Often patients find their way to the chapel and just sit quietly at the back for a few moments – something that I suspect most of them would never dream of doing in their normal lives. In subsequent conversations, I then often detect that they will be returning home with a renewed sense of inner peace and confidence. Clearly the exterior calm of the hospital, and the suspension of activity, plays a part in the achievement of this inward stillness. Whether they would think themselves to be religious or not, most probably not, quietness has helped put them in tune with the Divine. It is not just that they have had the leisure to think properly, the space itself has gently intimated something of the Reality beyond themselves.

To be human is to be busy, creatively engaged with plans and projects. But to be fully human, such activity must always be balanced with the reflection, contemplation and sheer passivity that silence allows. Speech is the systole and silence the diastole of our essential beings, action and rest our in-breathing and our out-breathing. Activity alone will ultimately become utterly meaningless if it is divorced from its source and from the One who is able to grant it value. We forget how much silence has been taken from us in urban life by the radio, television and car. To compensate for this, we have to search for silence, going on retreats or taking solitary walks, and this may seem rather contrived and artificial. But there is nothing more natural than silence – and no easier nor more direct means for sensitizing ourselves to that Divinity in relation to whom our humanity has full meaning.

We would do well to begin to follow through the implications of this appreciation; for example, it is interesting that evangelism usually consists of a very assertive verbalization. Obviously the

Christian faith has to be explained and argued for, but I wonder if this is always the manner in which to start. When St Paul addressed some curious Athenians in the Areopagus, he appealed to the immediacy and universality of God, and to their implicit awareness of him. God intended, he said, that they should seek him, 'in the hope that they might feel after him and find him. Yet he is not far from each one of us, for "In him we live and move and have our being"; as even some of your poets have said, "For we are indeed his offspring"' (Acts 17.28). Perhaps we ought more often to begin our evangelism by stimulating people to stop and listen to that which is already around them. Too often, Christians out to convert imagine that they possess a faith that the unconverted desperately need and completely lack. More often, the reality is that people will have already begun to feel after him and will have some sort of implicit awareness of God. We might arouse less defensiveness if we began by inviting them to take this awareness more seriously, attending to it with greater concentration, than by treating them as if they were spiritual morons, and ourselves hard-sell salesmen.

Such an approach to evangelism would proceed from the conviction that God is close to each one of us. Once a basic apprehension of this Presence had been discovered, *then* the framework of Christian belief could be introduced as the key to the Reality. So the evangelist might begin by gently but persistently prompting certain questions: 'Why is there something and not nothing?', 'Do love and the finer human qualities have a value beyond themselves?' 'Can you discern a purposive pattern emerging in your life?'. Doubtless questions like these are commonly asked. But perhaps the greatest service a Christian evangelist can provide is to encourage the opening up of an area of personal space in which the seeker can attend to the question and let the glimmerings of an answer begin to dawn. This requires great sensitivity, patience and self-control on the part of the evangelist, but the contemporary lack of interior space should not be underestimated. Busy-ness has invaded our souls and stunts our spiritual growth. It is the Church's key role to allow and authorize our taking time off from productive activity purely to ponder its deepest meaning.

The most effective way to teach is by example rather than by precept, so we must ensure that we are seen to be a listening and a pondering Church. Our church buildings tend naturally to be physically quiet. This is a quality that we should seek to enhance so that even casual visitors, when they enter them, are struck by a sacred and arresting silence. Where else in a modern town can this be found? Even art galleries and museums are often noisy places. Perhaps we should have the courage to advertise our church buildings as places where nothing happens – and nothing with a capital N! Surely we need, as never before, these still points in a turning world, allowing the possibility of a holy hiatus: gaps in the unrelenting pursuit of we know not what, where we catch an echo of that which alone endures: 'heard, half-heard, in the stillness/ Between two waves of the sea'.[1] It may of course be that the silence we carefully cultivate is then ignored and violated by the heedless who enter the building. In a small way, this may be part of our Christian suffering, accepted uncomplainingly. A peaceful if sad equanimity will soon return to the building.

The Christian Church still includes its contemplative religious orders, devoting their time to the daily round of the Opus Dei which reverberates constantly in the silence that is its context. Even Reformed Christians should see that these communities are really at the centre of the life of the Church, for they have most radically made the word the centre of their own lives. Far from being eccentric, they are the ones from who we should take our cue for they bear witness to a total orientation of the self to the mystery of God. They exist as a parable of the hidden but essential life of the Christian. The twentieth-century American Quaker, Thomas R. Kelly, describes the outward appearance of those in whom this orientation has become well established. 'These are not people of dallying idleness nor of obviously mooning meditation; they are busy carrying their full load as well as we, but . . . with quiet joy and springing step . . . poised and at peace. . . . Most of us, I fear, have not surrendered all else, in order to attend to the Holy Within.'[2]

> We scrabble in the dust,
> thinking to strain the dust for eternal gold.
> But you are here:
> form of the formed,
> breath of the breathing,
> presence of the quiet earth.

Traditionally, children have been taught to close their eyes when they pray, 'hands together, eyes closed'. Many adults continue the practice. Certainly this aids concentration, but does it imply that we have to shut out the world in order to concentrate on God? St John of the Cross thought so, for he said that only by 'blinding itself in its faculties ... the soul will see the light'.[3] In other words, one has to blind oneself to the created order in order to see with inward sight the uncreated light. By the same token, silent prayer has often been understood as the silencing of mundane experience so that a spiritual apprehension can be developed. This has not exactly been my approach, being unwilling to set aside or negate that range of experience through the five senses which is, to some extent, common to us all. I have a deep suspicion of the notion that we possess an inner spiritual faculty which somehow transcends ordinary experience. Rather, I would say that the spiritual is a particular qualitative evaluation of the latter. So it has been my aim to draw attention to that silence which is a natural feature of our world, and to stress the value of attaining a sympathetic stillness ourselves. This is not the denial, but a deep affirmation of the this-worldly, and it is with this evaluation that mundane experience can become a medium for the disclosure of God.

On the one hand, then, Christians should endorse that empiricism to which we are both intellectually heir and, if we are English, temperamentally inclined. Knowledge comes from the observation and analysis of the material world. Silence is one element of this data, and we should realize that it is a purely subjective judgement to say that silence represents a mere emptiness. It is not the word that is meaningful and silence meaningless. Continuous noise would be meaningless and requires silence before it can become expressive. Silence is an essential component of the physical structure of being. This may sound grandiloquent, but it is so easy to miss the silence. From time to time we should all get up early and listen quietly in that hour before the dawn chorus breaks. We ought to consider the immense distances that separate planets and stars in space, the almost imperceptible echo of the big bang fading to a most complete stillness. Silence is a real feature of the real world and deserves to be noticed.

On the other hand, those with a religious faith have their particular contribution to make to a critique of a strict empiricism. Our reliable knowledge does derive from observation and analysis of the material world, but we should beware of *under-interpreting* the data we receive. Part of our mental equipment consists of the imagination, and I am sure that we underestimate the extent to which this is used even in the most objective observation of data. The senses provide us with the raw data, our beliefs and ideas (sorted out rationally) are the means for their interpretation, but it is with the imagination that we synthesize these subjective and objective elements into a meaningful pattern of personal experience. Scientists have had occasion to remind themselves of the place of creative subjective thinking in their analytical work,[4] and by the same token we need to be aware of an interplay between data and belief in spiritual experience which is facilitated by the imagination. The content of Christian belief can be seen as the most glorious story, an ongoing saga into which we weave our own lives. We have the ability to appropriate the story for ourselves and to read ourselves into the plot. This does not mean that we make no effort to distinguish between fact and fantasy in religion, for both reason and the imagination have an indispensable role to play. We are able imaginatively to *enter into* our rationally held beliefs.

Silence has been presented as one datum of spiritual experience. But is is also an inherent quality of silence to stimulate the imagination. It fills us with anticipation (or apprehension); it suggests visions of harmony and calmness (or, at times, of anarchic chaos); it may intimate a presence (or absence). Entering an art gallery we are visually arrested and imaginatively stimulated by the paintings surrounding us. Entering a quiet church, or walking alone across a field at dead of night with the moon shining down upon us, the silence is similarly arresting and begins to engage our imagination. Indeed, a simple atmosphere of peace and stillness can be very powerful. We fill our churches with stained-glass windows and tangible representations of the faith. Filling the building with a prayerful silence can be even more dramatic. Merely as a contrast to constant noise, silence can stop us in our tracks and instantly refresh our aesthetic sensibilities.

By its very nature, then, silence often evokes an imaginative interpretation of itself. This helps to explain why we may come to appreciate it as a sort of natural sacrament of God's presence; it stimulates the perception of further meaning. But silence is not so much a door into another spiritual world, as a glass in which the spiritual nature of this world is glimpsed. If we cannot see the wood for the trees, we should not look somewhere else for the wood but more sensitively examine the trees. Christians are called to live most fully in this world, and not to denigrate, but to push the empirical sciences towards an ever-deeper discernment:

> Names for you we utter,
> each time grander and more fitting.
> These names, neither accepted nor rejected,
> sink deep into our minds,
> rooting in forgetfulness,
> until, suddenly, we are named!

Two basic principles have been growing and becoming plainer as we have explored the spiritual significance of silence. The first is that religious language is not simply descriptive of God in a static dispassionate manner; the second is that there can be no experience of God without beliefs. Religious language is essentially dynamic, and has no real meaning apart from our relationship with that of which it is an expression. This is no new insight. In the nineteenth century, Schleiermacher stated that language is entirely secondary to our feelings about God, and this statement has been very influential ever since:

> From within, in their original, characteristic form, the emotions of piety must issue. They must be indubitably your own feelings, and not mere stale descriptions of the feelings of others ... religion cannot and will not originate in the pure impulse to know. What we feel and are conscious of in religious emotions is not the nature of things, but their operation upon us.[5]

When we talk about God it is to express our feeling that 'our being and living is a being and living in and through God'. Such verbalization has its place, but Schleiermacher teaches us to see it as expressive of our *feeling* about God – which is the primary matter – and not simply as a plain objective description of God. As for he who has only religious ideas and no feeling for God, Schleiermacher says: 'His soul is barren in religious matters, and his ideas are merely supposititious children which he has adopted, in the secret feeling of his own weakness.' We ought certainly to agree with this emphasis on feeling. In our secular times, with the credibility of religious beliefs being everywhere questioned, we survive by relying more heavily on the dimension of personal experience. But mere ideas about God have always been, on their own, sterile and insufficient apart from a living faith in him. True religion is not about the handling and systematic arrangement of ideas, but is rather a dynamic personal engagement with the eternal life-giver.

However, we have, I hope, developed a more even-handed understanding of the relationship between beliefs and experience here, and will want to challenge the cerebral bias in religion which suggests that they are completely distinct. Schleiermacher's emphasis on experience is fine, bringing the dead forms of religion alive and putting them firmly in their place. But he introduces an imbalance into our thinking if we are not careful. Religious language will have meaning only in proportion to our feeling for God, yes, but there can be no intelligible feelings without language, for there is a necessary symbiotic relationship of interdependence between experience and belief. Experience consists of the *interpretation* of data, and therefore beliefs are quite indispensable. Certainly an increased emphasis on the value of personal experience is required: it reawakens us to the fact that faith is a total response of body, mind and spirit to a living God. But we must beware of the creeping assumption that there is a direct and immediate access to God which stands apart from the formalism of religious traditions. It is tempting to suppose that we possess some 'inner light' by which we are able to hold an intuitive communion with God. But this would involve a delusion similar to that of imagining the mind to be an entity which can exist independently of the chemical processes of our physical brains. If only it could be shown to be so! We would then be liberated from the fear of senility and death and all the other finite limitations of a merely physical organ. But although the myth of an immortal soul continues to hold some sway, the ageing process rather suggests that the spirit is simply the brain thinking spiritually. I simply *am* a body, and there is no alchemy for turning body into pure soul. Similarly, experience of God cannot be separated from actual cultural religious forms. Without the latter, spiritual data must remain totally unintelligible.

This realization is a bit disappointing, for it means that we are stuck with the Church with all its warts and bumps and funny ways. But it is an optimistically realistic position rather than a nihilistic one. Acknowledgement of our physicality leads, if not to despair, to a radical faith in the resurrection of our mortal selves. We have to accept that death is the natural end of our natural lives, and therefore that a new life beyond death is simply and wholly the gift of God. We cannot understand what this new life will be, but can only trust, utterly, in the life-giver. Through this faith we take it that our present, inherently limited, life is an indication of what shall be. Lived dynamically, that is, with faith in the resurrection of Christ, our present life provides us with sufficient confidence about the hereafter. The same gap between this life and the resurrection, and the same potential for a sufficient faith in the latter by those still in the former, exists between human religious traditions and the reality of God. It is true that acceptance of the indispensability of beliefs in personal experience means that such experience is a closed, circular process. It is meaningless to suggest that we could ever break free from our particular interpretative framework and find God as he is in himself. But we do trust in the reality of God beyond our conceptions – and indeed feel that in our experience it is God who reaches out to us rather than the other way about. Our present experience, again inherently limited, provides us with a sufficient confidence in tne reality of God when we make our faith dynamic. This dynamism comes with the profound assimilation of beliefs into that tacit form whereby it is as if we *live* them; when the use of them in making experience becomes so familiar to us that it feels more like intuition than thinking. It is precisely when we are able to 'forget' our beliefs in this way, that we are most receptive to seeing the ordinary, in the visionary words of Gerard Manley Hopkins, 'charged with the grandeur of God'. Then a thoroughly human system of ideas surges with Divine energy.

In past generations, Christian beliefs were readily assimilated through constant rehearsal at home, school and church. In our less religious days, such beliefs have a strangeness and distinctiveness since they are no longer known and accepted unquestioningly by the majority of the population. We believers are aware of their novelty and are naturally self-conscious of our acceptance of them. Being constantly in conflict with a-religious or atheistic views makes it hard for us to forget and assimilate our beliefs. Continually we are called upon to justify our position. But an overt Christianity is raw and immature. It separates us from the world and prevents us from appreciating natural sacraments of God. We remain spiritual infants, sitting on the floor playing with our alphabet cards and never growing up to become fluent in the language of profound human discourse.

This self-consciousness affects the way we worship and the

manner in which we teach the Christian faith. We are always trying to *explain*. Modern liturgy is set out in an orderly style, with headings and sub-headings. The language echoes the stilted sing-song of the school assembly: 'Good morning, everyone', 'Good morning, teacher'; 'The Lord be with you', 'And also with you'; 'You are God and we praise you ...'. Many of us who are enthusiastic advocates of liturgical renewal have none the less come to realize that the language of modern Anglican liturgy somehow fails to resonate. Do we not need a text that is more poetic and aesthetically engaging, more evocative of hidden meanings than instantly explanatory? Perhaps one reason we find it hard to include silence in the liturgy is that a flow of superficial words does not exactly prompt us to stop and ponder? There again, perhaps we simply try to use too many words in our weekly hour of worship and a smaller quantity with a greater amount of silence would begin to resonate more? There has to be a prominent place for worship that the totally uninitiated will find accessible. But we also need a liturgy that we can get into the bloodstream of regular worshippers – songs with a timeless rhythm and prayers with a haunting elusiveness, which vibrate rather than seem discontinuous with the rest of our lives.

The urgent need for a thorough integration into our beliefs, and the cultivation of an informed Christian understanding, does not go unrecognized. Many dioceses now have excellent schemes of adult Christian education. Often these are modelled on the Open University modular approach. One can choose to follow a series of learning units about the New Testament, or prayer, or church history for example. But the danger with this self-contained method of learning is that we will merely skate over the surface of a variety of topics, ending our learning with the last session of the course. The problem lies not with this form of education but with the learners, for we tend to have an inbuilt cultural resistance to being immersed long and deep in a Christian world-view. It is such a commitment that needs to be recovered. Short bursts of study are no substitute for a slow continuous reading of the Bible, a questioning of and being questioned by the text, a serious pondering on the mystery of God. We need to place more emphasis on the formation of Christian character, the thorough cultivation of spiritual consciousness. We must have clearly enunciated beliefs at hand with which to answer our critics, but it is more important that we *use* these beliefs in the process of engaging with God himself:

> We want to hear the message,
> and we want to preach it boldly.
> We want the substance, the reward,
> a reason for the effort.
> We want, we want.
> Silence is the message, for what we *need*
> is to wait.

As a priest I sometimes feel frightened and oppressed by the Church: oppressed because it is a self-justifying, all-consuming monster; frightened because we seem to forget its only reason for existing – which is to proclaim the reality of God. These negative feelings stem not from a sense that we neglect our task of proclamation, but from our being all too keen to promote it. So much of our effort seems to be that of hoping to sell to the world our Divine product that we are blind to the violence we do to the object of our faith in the process. As a Church our structures and our language ought to reflect, as faithfully as possible, the nature of God as we experience him. If our God is haunting and elusive, offering us no certainties bar the sense of an inexhaustible love, waiting for us to respond and grow before he reveals more of himself, then this should be reflected in the life of our Church. The Church is a means to an end and we must ensure that the means are appropriate for, and in sympathy with, that end. If God is patient with us, then the Church too must be long-suffering; if God does not impose himself on us then we should have, quite publicly, a radical commitment to waiting in hope.

If the Church were thus more consciously to make itself the arena for God's silence, then I believe some profound changes in its outward appearance would occur. Three examples may be isolated from what would inevitably be a very subtle process of change. In the first place, the significance of personal experience would be more highly valued – but more *honestly* pursued. The quality of personal experience will always have a high priority in organized religion because faith can never be sustained merely by ideas and ceremonial. Currently, however, we may ask how much corporately fostered personal experience is really any more than a synthetic wish-fulfilment? The Church often seems to feel that its task is to give people something to fill the emptiness of their inner world. It can offer the certainties of dogmatic belief, the emotionalism of charismatic worship, or simply a churchly love of the institution itself. But these will ultimately prove to be malnourishing substitutes for the sustenance that a fully human spirituality requires. The faces of people at worship are a real give-away, whether it be ecstatic ones in a sea of swaying uplifted hands, or those with eyes shut tight as the venerable words of the Book of Common Prayer flow on. Ministers and those rude enough to look around at the congregation will often notice the strained expression of contrived worship. In the long term, the Church is doing people a disservice, for what we most urgently need is not a comforter to fill the barrenness, but the strength and encouragement to attend to our inner emptiness. Clearly taught and thoroughly pondered beliefs are the key with which to interpret this emptiness, but they must not become an evasion from it. This will never be a popular approach, for it leads to a worship that is the antithesis of slickness – fragmentary with but the occasional morsel of meaning – but it allows us to engage with the reality of ourselves and with the reality of our God.

In the second place, the Church that allows God's silence to fill it will take down the institutional turnstiles for those who wish to enter. If we meet a God who does not impose himself, but quietly elicits the fullest response by way of an unconditional grace, then we are hardly in the business of ensuring that new subscribers meet conditions. It is, for example, tempting and conscience-salving to expect parents who want their children to be baptized to conform to our expectations of church attendance, and to demand that divorced people who wish to be remarried in church submit themselves to our scrutiny. But if God does not deal with us like this, we have not the right to treat others so. Perhaps the only condition we ought to lay down for such people is that when they come to their parish church they are inwardly quiet and open to the reality of God. Of course, the silence will be meaningless without the beliefs to interpret it, but it is the very silence of the Divine presence that may make them receptive *to* belief. In preparation for a baptism or a wedding, the priest will do a great deal of *talking*, but it is equally important that time is given to a serious exploration of the feelings of the individuals concerned. It is our role to encourage them to listen to themselves. Then, when they come to the service itself, if there are a few

opportunities created for quiet reflection, these will be a continuation of the same process. It is most valuable if people can be
brought to the sacraments in a thoughtful frame of mind, open to the
God who is open to them.

Then, in the third place, we must understand that by its very
nature the Church has in turn to be assertive and visible, *and* silent
and invisible. Its nature is to be a sacrament of the Kingdom of God,
that is, both pointing to and a means for God's inauguration of a new
order. Participation in the life of a local church is (at its best) a
foretaste of the Kingdom; its worship, love, forgiveness, and
struggle for peace and justice in the world are birthpangs of the
Kingdom. In many respects, the new order is at odds with the old
and this means that the Church is called to be prophetic, its
members openly challenging the values and priorities of present
society. The gospel has to be preached, loud and clear, and its
implications laid bare for all to see. It is vital that the Church is seen,
with a high public profile, to *be* the Church. But the elements of a
sacrament are ordinary things invested with an extraordinary
significance. In the Eucharist, bread and wine become the body and
blood of Christ, but we can still go home for dinner and eat bread
and drink wine. A sacrament is a particular event mediating and
proclaiming a general truth. Jesus is present in the Eucharist – but
also at all times and in all places. The extraordinary symbol springs
from the ordinary, but then merges into the background again. The
Church does not lose its potency as a sacrament if its members spend
nine-tenths of their time in non-Church activities. Indeed, to have
any effect the sacrament has to be invested and applied, the
Kingdom of God comes by way of politics, commerce and plain
unglamorous human caring. It is an awful temptation simply to
continue to massage the Church institution and never to engage with
that emerging reality of which it is a sacrament. So we need to learn
to be happy with ourselves as, at times, a silent and invisible Church.
This can be emotionally difficult and it poses the hard question,
'What is it most important for me to be doing when I am not being
churchly?' In our society we have lots of silent, anonymous
Christians, and we have a smaller number of assertive ones; we need
more who can be in turn both assertive and wholly silent.

But, O, the emptiness of your namelessness.
Against you we rail:

O cry of the forsaken,
vain hope of the hopeless,
bitterness of the despairing,
begging bowl of the dying;
we lash out,
and your bruised body twitches.

Recent decades have witnessed the production of a huge number of
books about prayer. There is clearly a steady religious market. But it
is one thing to dip into the latest paperback of popular spirituality,
and quite another earnestly to pursue a practical commitment to a
life of prayer. Such a commitment involves a hard grind with long
stretches where the going seems very hard. Similarly, it is all very
fine to write edifyingly about the profound value of silence in prayer,
but when the person who struggles to pray actually encounters it, the
silence may seem cruel, inexplicable and dark. Writing about
prayer, and perhaps particularly about silence in prayer, seems to
invite the most high flown of sentiments, but such aspirations will
only nourish the spirit if they are rooted firmly in the harsh realities
of our human condition! 'Be still and know that I am God', we quote
encouragingly. Yes, but also, 'Be still and know the pain of loss of
meaning and lack of God's presence'. Both will be encountered by
the one who enters honestly into the prayer of silence: this medium
of God is a bitter-sweet reality, and if the sweetness is very sweet
then the bitterness can be unexpectedly bitter.

What happens when we refrain from using customary religious
words and conventional images in prayer is the resurgence of deep
inner feelings and nascent personal images. Now it may be that
much of this material is entirely negative – the very stuff of our
nightmares. We may feel that the rising forces of angst and
alienation threaten to suffocate us. In the first place, we have to
accept this fear of ourselves, but then in the second place, learn how
to baptize it. The first *is* terribly hard, and the more sincerely we try
to be 'good', the harder and more frightening it is, for our deeper
feelings become less and less acceptable. Indeed, the attempt to be
good seems to goad our darker area into life. Jung recognized this:
'the more Christian one's consciousness is, the more heathenishly
does the unconscious behave'. But then he goes on to add, 'if in the
rejected heathenism there are values which are important for life'.[6]
We assume too quickly that the more hidden parts of ourselves,

which in silence begin to be manifested, are all thoroughly bad and rotten and must be repressed if they cannot be rejected altogether. As Jung said of Christians, 'The doctrine that all evil thoughts come from the heart and that the human soul is a sink of iniquity must lie deep in the marrow of their bones.'[7] But if Christians believe in the goodness of creation, then they must believe in the goodness of their own creation – even if there *are* some frightening elements below the threshold of consciousness. It becomes possible to accept our whole selves when we can believe that God loves us, and is present, even in the depths and bowels of ourselves.

Once we can at least accept these fears about ourselves, and begin to feel that it might not be totally life-threatening to allow silence to loosen the door upon our inner cave of wriggling demons, their baptism becomes possible. In our 'rejected heathenism' there *will* be 'values which are important for life'. The baptismal candidate must naturally feel exposed and vulnerable when called upon to make a profession of faith, be stripped of his old ways and then plunged under the waters. The embarrassingly public nature of the ceremony reflects the painful act of opening one's whole self to God, owning all that had rather been thrust down out of sight and covered over. But as the baptismal waters symbolically come right up over the head, and the old man is drowned, so the whole of one's being is finally allowed to come into contact with the Divine. All is exposed and the vulnerability becomes a therapeutic hurt. Jung teaches us that the primeval mud of our unconscious is actually a rich resource for new life. If silent prayer makes us feel vulnerable to darker forces within ourselves, then we have to see this not as a problem but as the potential for our salvation. God seeks to enter our very selves. Or rather, the moment for our recognizing God as already present in our deepest selves has arrived. This realization, and the acceptance of all that we are, allows our complete Christianization. Jung is right, 'Too few people have experienced the divine image as the innermost possession of their own souls.'[8]

But the God we find may not be the one we want or even expect. In times of personal crisis, or when we stand helplessly beside the sufferings of others, we pray for a God who will *act*. But what we find, and that only if we are patient, is simply the bruised body of his presence. We meet the One who suffers in our suffering; in the darkness we stumble against the crucified whose passivity has mysteriously and disappointingly not yet been succeeded in the victory of the resurrection, for he still 'opens not his mouth'. Perhaps it is time that we Christians openly confessed that we do not have a complete theodicy. We cannot solve the enigma of pain and wasteful suffering in the light of our faith in a loving Father. But then, it is sometimes only when we angrily reject this faith that, in our bitterness, we truly encounter him. Personal suffering leaves us, so often, the shipwrecked survivors of a religious system. We cling to a few spars in the grey heaving seas and the lashing rain. We can identify with the Lord's words to St Paul, 'My grace is sufficient for you, for my power is made perfect in weakness' (2 Cor. 12.9). But we have to see that God does not stand apart from this weakness, but instead clothes himself with it. His power is made perfect in his solidarity with the weakness of suffering humankind. Quite how the Divine power could ever be said to find perfection by way of an utter indentification with human weakness is a question that takes the whole of our life experience, and more, to begin to be answered. What we can say, and this is wonderful enough, is that God's grace is indeed *sufficient* for us. The bare fact that in the midst of personal devastation we can discern the co-suffering of the crucified God is little enough, but strangely, *is* enough. The grace of this presence sustains us – at least giving us the strength to ask 'Why?' – and keeps us travelling on.

> Tears drying, uncertain peace returns.
> Unlocking hardened hearts,
> stilling, with a single outstretched arm
> all the winds and waves.
> The empty heart opened
> echoes to an eternal silence –
> like finding like!
> Peace passing understanding: home.

Silence keeps alive a priority that is continually in danger of being forgotten in all human theologizing: that is, to let God be God. In both cult and thought we prefer a God we can handle. We feel we need to know how to become familiar with the One we worship, to know comfortably how our needs and desires can be harmonized with what his purposes might be for us. So we domesticate and anthropomorphize our glimpses of the Divine reality into something on a more human scale, a household god. This is an insidious process as we gradually mould the vision of God into an image suited to our own purposes. Prayer becomes little more than a dialogue with the self; holiness is converted into self-improvement on our own terms. There are times when this gentle prattle about God with such a dangerous tendency needs to be radically silenced. Strictly speaking, we cannot have *experience* of God beyond the range of those beliefs we use in its interpretation. But we can be aware that there is an infinitely greater reality beyond our limited experience. This must always be the context for our knowing, thinking, and speaking of God. When we open a book of theology, or when we come to Holy Communion, we should approach in awe and wonder – like Moses ascending Mount Sinai and finding the Divine mystery wrapped in fire and smoky darkness. Words addressed to God, in worship or in speculative thought, ought always consciously to be uttered into this silence of the transcendent. Western Christianity needs to recover the fierceness with which this principle continues to be maintained in Eastern Orthodoxy.

However, there is something ultimately satisfying to be discovered in the practice of silent prayer. In it we touch the essence of our being for, in the most profound sense, it is true to say that we were born out of silence and that we shall eventually die back into it. By this I mean the *raison de' être* of our humanity is with God, and our true end consists in integration with him. To speak of humankind having an 'end' is not, though, a popular notion. Perhaps the nearest thing to it for many people is the assumption that their aim in this life should be to realize as much personal potential as possible, to find self-fulfilment. But the fragility of human life, highly vulnerable to illness, the behaviour of others and the mutability of our natural environment, should serve to warn us of the inadequacy of this assumption. Aristotle, on whom so much modern thought is founded, provides us with a firmer basis. He taught that humankind has an end, a *telos*, which is *eudaimonia* – usually rather crudely translated as 'happiness' or 'well-being'. The function for which we exist, by way of which we shall know a true fullness of being, he describes as 'an activity of soul in accordance with goodness'; indeed, 'in accordance with the best and most complete form of goodness'.[9] Aristotle identifies 'speculative activity' as the most complete form of goodness: those engaged in it will have the most complete lives. This is so because 'the intellect more than anything else is the man'. However, by 'speculation', Aristotle does not mean the search for truth, but rather its contemplation. This most vital activity requires stillness, for 'there is an activity not only of movement but of immobility, like that of thought'. Its enjoyment (in the deepest sense of the word) is what grants us the sense of most complete well-being, 'those who have knowledge pass their time more pleasantly than those who are engaged in its pursuit'.

From a very different culture, predating Christianity, Aristotle nevertheless recalls us to the essential significance of our humanity. We are to recognize that our true end is purely and simply to contemplate the truth. This will bring us the greatest sense of completeness and happiness. Now as Christians we can, by grace, name this truth as the mystery of God himself. We can also explore the range of the term 'contemplation', seeing that it has a dynamic meaning and is not merely a description of the individual sitting alone in meditation. We are called to live the whole of our lives contemplatively, discerning the wonder of an ultimately unknowable God's interaction with us and allowing ourselves to be woven into *his* dynamic. Neither can our authentic *telos* be replaced with a mere self-fulfilment without doing violence to ourselves: the latter will lead us into a cul-de-sac of eternal dissatisfaction and world-weariness without our ever knowing why. Silence opens us to the realization that the full value of humankind does not lie in itself, but in the contemplation of God – and to the discovery that this entails nothing less than a thorough integration with the Divine.

> Hush, be still.
> Impregnated with silence
> we carry
> the Word.

For so many of us the word 'God' is a noun we no longer know what to do with. Its meaning has a 'dazzling darkness' which moves, but does not illuminate, the human spirit. For many, to attempt to pray is to stumble into a desert of dry bones. The winds of traditional belief whistle eerily around and there is a disconcerting presence of absence. At times, if the attempt is pursued, something shifts in the depths of our being – but we know not what. The message of this book has been that the correspondence that can thus often be felt between an actual and an inner silence is not to be fled from. Sometimes silence is disturbing, at other times it may be deeply restful, but always it has the potential to become both the means for and the actual occasion of a sacramental disclosure of God. It is, perhaps more than has been appreciated, the most appropriate form of prayer for our age. The passivity of silence challenges our restless acquisitiveness with a radical call to wait in emptiness. If we are more than ever aware of the merely provisional validity that religious beliefs can have, then we are invited to commit ourselves to them *as if they were* absolutely true. It will be the personal experience that results, as they are used to interpret data, that will breathe new life into traditional religious systems for us.

In the earlier part of one's spiritual development prayer is often direct, affirmative, and wonderfully satisfying. We speak to God in the intimacy of our hearts and feel that he answers and stays alongside us at all times. For some, this sense of God will be be sustained, more or less, for the rest of their lives. But for others prayer unaccountably turns sour. They no longer feel God's presence, the word indeed loses its first meaning. The ordinary mundane world looms large and the spiritual seems just a fantasy. If they try to pray, they no longer know what to say, or think. The inward meaningfulness seems to have dried up. They (or rather *we*, for is this not our experience?) then need to be told that this is not the end of prayer but its beginning. It is precisely when we have, for the time being, used up our intellectual and emotional resources and are empty that we can be open to the Divine mystery. The secret is to stay with the emptiness and gradually to let our apparently dissipated beliefs inform this silence. The mystics of the Church have characteristically stressed the hardness of this way. It is easier, believe me, to write about than to practise! It is a way that requires us to be ruthlessly realistic – to the extent of being open to the ultimate reality. It *fills* us unknowingly with the Unknown.

The Quaker Thomas R. Kelly may be allowed the final word. He articulated that invitation which is addressed to us all: 'Hasten unto him who calls you in the silences of your heart'. There *are* moments when the ordinary becomes the gate of heaven, 'when the Presence *steals upon us*, all unexpected, not the product of agonized effort, as we live in a new dimension of life'. This new dimension invites us into an ever-greater plenitude of silence. Kelly testifies that such enlightenment is at once simple and profound, natural, and the result of God's grace as we then move on, 'stilled, tranquil, in childlike trust listening to Eternity's whisper, walking with a smile into the dark'.[10]

Notes

1 'Little Gidding', in T. S. Eliot, *Four Quartets*. London, Faber & Faber, 1944.
2 R. T. Kelly, 'Testament of Devotion', in D. Steere, ed., *Quaker Spirituality*. London, SPCK, 1984, p. 304.
3 John of the Cross, *The Ascent of Mount Carmel*, trans. E. Allison Peers, London, Burns & Oates, 1983, II.IV.6.
4 See T. Kuhn, *The Structure of Scientific Revolutions*, International Encyclopaedia of Unified Science. Chicago, University of Chicago, 1962, vol. 2.
5 'Second Speech', in F. Schleiermacher, *On Religion, Speeches to Its Cultured Despisers*, trans. J. Oman. New York, Harper & Row, 1958, pp. 27-8.
6 C. G. Jung, 'Answer to Job', in *Psychology and Religion: East and West*. London, Ark, 1958-69, p. 713.
7 C. G. Jung, *Psychology and Alchemy*. London, Routledge, 1953–8, p. 126.
8 ibid., p. 12.
9 Aristotle, *Nichomachean Ethics*, trans. J. A. K. Thomson, Harmondsworth, Penguin Classics, 1953, p. 39–40.
10 Kelly, 'Testament of Devotion', p. 289.

Index